They Don't Tell the Truth
About the Wind

They Don't Tell the Truth
About the Wind

Hands-On Explorations in K-3 Science

Marilyn Fleer, Tim Hardy,
Karen Baron, & Cliff Malcolm

In collaboration with
Curriculum Corporation

HEINEMANN
Portsmouth, NH

Heinemann
A division of Reed Elsevier Inc.
361 Hanover Street
Portsmouth, NH 03801-3912
Offices and agents throughout the world

First published 1995 by
Curriculum Corporation
St Nicholas Place
141 Rathdowne St
Carlton Vic 305 3
Australia

Library of Congress Cataloging-in-Publication Data
They don't tell the truth about the wind : hands-on
explorations in K-3 science / Marilyn Fleer . . . [et al.]
in collaboration with Curriculum Corporation.
       p.   cm.
   ISBN 0-435-08374-0
   1. Science—Study and teaching (Early
childhood)—Australia.   2. Active learning—
Australia.   3. Storytelling—Australia.
I. Fleer, Marilyn.   II. Curriculum Corporation
(Australia)
LB1139.5.S35T44   1996
372.3049—dc20   95-35550
                                           CIP

This publication uses outcomes from *Science—a
curriculum profile for Australian schools*. Permission has
been given by the publisher, Curriculum Corporation.
To have a full understanding of the profile, it is
advised that it be read in its entirety. *Science—a
curriculum profile for Australian schools* is also available
from Heinemann.

Editor: Victoria Merecki
Production: Renée Nicholls
Text design: Joni Doherty
Cover design: Jenny Jensen Greenleaf
Cover illustration: Mary Sims

Printed in the United States of America on
acid-free paper

99 98 97 96 VG 1 2 3 4 5 6 7 8 9

Contents

ACKNOWLEDGMENTS vii

INTRODUCTION 1

Scientists in the Kitchen 9
IDENTIFYING NATURAL AND PROCESSED MATERIALS

Cycles of Life 17
LIVING, GROWING, AND DYING

The Dark is a Big Shadow 27
UNDERSTANDING NIGHT AND DAY

If the Cow Runs Out of Grass, She Stops 37
ENERGY AND FUEL

The Scientific Birthday Party 41
STATES AND PROPERTIES OF MATTER

The Teddy Bears' Barbecue 51
CHEMICAL CHANGE

Egbert, What Do You Know About Rain? ... 59
THE WATER CYCLE

A Watery Treasure Hunt 69
FLOATING AND SINKING

Oh No, Quickie the Cat Dissolved! 75
DISSOLVING

How Do You Make Hard Vegetables Soft? .. 81
HEAT AND ENERGY

The Zoo in My Garden 89
ANIMALS, PLANTS, AND HABITATS

Pop Goes the Corn 97
PROCESSING MATERIALS

My Special Flashlight 105
ILLUMINATION AND ELECTRICITY

Mechanical Toys 115
HOW DO THEY WORK?

Making Dirt 123
EARTH AND SOIL

The Story Within 133
WHAT'S INSIDE YOUR BODY?

Our Place in Space 141
OUTER SPACE

They Don't Tell the Truth About
the Wind 145
WORKING SCIENTIFICALLY

Acknowledgments

They Don't Tell the Truth About the Wind was developed with support from Telecom Australia and the Commonwealth Department of Industry, Science and Technology. The authors also received a research grant from the University of Canberra to investigate children's scientific understanding.

We thank especially the many children who talked to us about their ideas and their interests and who gave us permission to use their drawings and quote their words. We dedicate the book to them.

The teachers who so generously gave their ideas and expertise are listed below, by unit. We greatly enjoyed working with them in creating the units, trying them out, and revising them.

SCIENTISTS IN THE KITCHEN: Allyson Davis, Wiradjuri Preschool Childcare Centre, ACT; Marion Prettyman, Rokeby Primary School, Tasmania; Lynda Bell, Waimea Heights School, ACT.

CYCLES OF LIFE: Shirley Gollings and Veronica Cleary, Giralang Primary School, ACT. Figures 5 and 6 are from an unpublished conference paper by K. Baron, and B. Gray, "Scaffolding Genres in Early Childhood Education," presented to the 1993 Literacy and Education Research Network Conference in collaboration with Genre III, University of Technology, Sydney, May 21–23, 1993.

THE DARK IS A BIG SHADOW: Vivien Smith and Sue Engel, Lyneham Primary School, ACT; Rhonda Christian, University of Canberra Curriculum Resources Centre.

IF THE COW RUNS OUT OF GRASS, SHE STOPS: Wendy Jobling, Syndal South Primary School, Victoria; Telsa Rudd and Daryl Francis, Huntingtower School, Victoria.

THE SCIENTIFIC BIRTHDAY PARTY: Wendy Lupton and Allyson Davis, Wiradjuri Preschool Childcare Centre, ACT; Kerry Kasmira, Stirling School, Northern Territory; Susan Adams, Glen Huon Primary School, Tasmania; Andrew Jones, Curriculum Support Officer, Hartz District, Tasmania.

THE TEDDY BEARS' BARBECUE: Careen Leslie, Wiradjuri Preschool Childcare Centre, ACT.

EGBERT, WHAT DO YOU KNOW ABOUT RAIN?: Cathy Halkett, Wiradjuri Preschool Childcare Centre, ACT; Judy Lowry, Huonville Primary School, Tasmania.

A WATERY TREASURE HUNT: Cathy Halkett, Wiradjuri Preschool Childcare Centre, ACT; Karen Watson, Theodore Preschool, ACT.

OH NO, QUICKIE THE CAT DISSOLVED!: Cathy Halkett, Wiradjuri Preschool Childcare Centre, Canberra; Marion Prettyman, Rokeby Primary School, Tasmania.

HOW DO YOU MAKE HARD VEGETABLES SOFT?: Marita Corra, Yarralumla Preschool, ACT.

THE ZOO IN MY GARDEN: Karina Sargeson, Holt Primary School, ACT; Marita Corra, Yarralumla Preschool, ACT.

POP GOES THE CORN: Ann Emerson-Elliott, Calwell Preschool, ACT.

MY SPECIAL FLASHLIGHT: Jan Elliot, Hughes Primary School, ACT; Karina Sargeson, Wiradjuri Preschool Childcare Centre, ACT; Patricia Hills, Campbell Street Primary, ACT; Sarah Jarvis, Huonville Primary School, Tasmania.

MECHANICAL TOYS: Julie McLaren, Florey Primary School, ACT.

MAKING DIRT: Wendy Jobling, Syndal South Primary School, Victoria; Telsa Rudd and Daryl Francis, Huntingtower School, Victoria.

THE STORY WITHIN: Careen Leslie, Wiradjuri Preschool Childcare Centre, ACT; Julie McLaren, Wiradjuri Preschool Childcare Centre, ACT.

OUR PLACE IN SPACE: Amy Vermeer and Karina Sargeson, Holt Primary School, ACT.

THEY DON'T TELL THE TRUTH ABOUT THE WIND: Vivien Smith and Sue Engel, Lyneham Primary School, ACT; Rhonda Christian, University of Canberra Curriculum Resources Centre, ACT.

Thanks also to Carol Linney and Cynthia Hayden, who transcribed audio- and videotapes, Louise Bannister, for secretarial help, Annette Mulhall, for helping with the artwork, and Sue Corrigan and Rhonda Christian, for preparing the planning and teaching resources.

Introduction

They Don't Tell the Truth About the Wind is a child-centered program for students ages four through eight years old. It is designed to help children make sense of their experience, build meaning, and take effective action in their world. The units describe classroom techniques for finding out what ideas, experiences and questions children have and building from there. The contexts in which ideas and skills are developed have been carefully chosen to be rewarding and relevant to children.

The units use a number of strategies for teaching, learning, and classroom management—small-group work, whole-class discussions, family involvement, role plays and puppet plays, text and equipment, field trips, brainstorming, problem solving, demonstration, film. This variety stems partly from the range of children's learning styles and partly from the kinds of things the children are learning.

Units run three to six weeks, depending on the time given to them each week and the backgrounds and interests of the children. Each unit has a unifying theme, or plot—a story, a problem to solve, questions and concerns. This sense of story in each unit enables the children to see from the start where the unit is headed, helping them to integrate their experiences and take a greater role in managing their own learning.

These explorations have been developed by the Curriculum Corporation in Australia and were extensively field-tested with early childhood teachers as well as children in child-care centers, preschools, and junior primary classrooms throughout Australia. The examples of student work that appear throughout were compiled from those field tests.

The program provides comprehensive coverage of the concepts

outlined in *A Statement on Science for Australian Schools and Science—A Curriculum Profile for Australian Schools*. The science statement and the profile are two of sixteen documents, commissioned by the Australian Education Council, that represent the results of a five-year, national collaborative curriculum development project. Each statement and profile combination addresses one of eight different areas of learning. The eight statements aim to provide a framework for curriculum development in each of those eight areas. The corresponding profiles are designed to improve teaching and learning and to provide a common language for reporting student achievement. The profiles and statements are linked—the profiles show the typical progression in achieving learning outcomes, while the statements are a framework of what might be taught to achieve those outcomes.

Each profile is divided into *strands*—the major elements of learning for the particular subject area. The strands are further broken down into *organizers* that describe the content, process, and/or conceptual understanding addressed in the strand. Finally, each strand consists of eight *achievement levels* that correspond to the typical progression in student learning.

The science profile strands, organizers, and achievement levels that are the focus of the units in *They Don't Tell the Truth About the Wind* are included here following this introduction. Every unit integrates ideas and skills across a number of strands. Furthermore, in an effort to challenge all of the children in a group and give each child an opportunity to make learning progress, every unit spans at least two levels in the profile. Many units indicate links to other curriculum areas; in some cases those links are developed in detail.

Using the Units

We expect and encourage you to use the units to suit your physical and organizational environment and the needs of your students. Since implementation and instruction will fall largely to you, we have designed the program to help you:

- The units are in two groups: the first group spans levels 1 and 2 of the science profile, the second group spans levels 1, 2, and 3. (In the trials, we found that a number of children are reaching level 3 by age eight but that most are still working at level 2.)
- The activities described are open-ended. They can be done in different ways, depending on the children. You can adjust them to suit your class.
- The units are told as stories, often in the words of teachers and children. We wanted to provide a sense of what some teachers have done with the units and the sorts of things their children said and produced. We also wanted you to see enough of the trial setting and the teachers' thinking to be able to make necessary modifications.

- Every unit includes a clear statement of the intended outcomes, the levels of the profile addressed, and the logic and activities that make up the unit.
- We have included explanations of the science involved, sometimes in a teacher's words, sometimes through examples of children's work, and sometimes as a sidebar to the text.
- Particular teaching approaches, like involving parents, using puppets, mapping concepts, and questioning, are described in detail in some units but not others. In this sense, the examples carry over from one unit to another. For instance, the approach to home-school involvement in *The Dark Is a Big Shadow* can readily be used in other units. The same is true for the language approach in *Cycles of Life*, the puppet used in *Egbert*, *What Do You Know About Rain?*, the local resources in *The Zoo in My Garden*, and so on.

Our fundamental assumption as we developed and wrote these explorations has been that teachers in preschool and primary school are typically highly skilled in organizing and managing learning experiences for young children. What they need is a set of science activities through which they can apply their teaching skills. Teaching science, in many respects, is no different from, say, teaching language or mathematics. With the support of a program like this, your children can learn about science enjoyably and successfully.

Working Scientifically

Every unit highlights aspects of working scientifically: the children are able to develop their process skills and to experience what it means to work scientifically as opposed to unscientifically. The final unit, "They Don't Tell the Truth About the Wind," draws together all aspects of working scientifically and allows children to reflect specifically on what that means. We recommend that you place it at or near the end of your program so that it can build on experience in other units.

Developing Your Own Program

While this book is a whole science program, you still need to make it your own. We expect and encourage you to adapt the units to your particular group of children, your physical and organizational environment, the location and community within which you live, and your own teaching style. You will also want to establish links between the units, particularly if you are organizing a complete program in a primary school.

You can follow the order of the units in this book, but there are many other possible arrangements. Examples are shown in Tables 1 and 2.

UNIT KINDERGARTEN
  1 Scientists in the Kitchen
  2 The Scientific Birthday Party
  3 How Do You Make Hard Vegetables Soft?
  4 A Teddy Bear Barbecue

FIRST GRADE
  1 The Story Within
  2 Egbert, What Do You Know About Rain?
  3 They Don't Tell the Truth About the Wind
  4 Oh No, Quickie the Cat Dissolved!
  5 A Watery Treasure Hunt

SECOND GRADE
  1 The Dark Is a Big Shadow
  2 Our Place in Space
  3 My Special Flashlight
  4 If the Cow Runs Out of Grass, She Stops

THIRD GRADE
  1 Mechanical Toys
  2 Pop Goes the Corn
  3 The Zoo in My Garden
  4 Cycles of Life
  5 Making Dirt

Table 1

UNIT KINDERGARTEN
  1 A Watery Treasure Hunt
  2 The Story Within
  3 Cycles of Life
  4 If the Cow Runs Out of Grass, She Stops

FIRST GRADE
  1 They Don't Tell the Truth About the Wind
  2 A Teddy Bear Picnic
  3 How Do You Make Hard Vegetables Soft?
  4 Oh No, Quickie the Cat Dissolved!
  5 The Dark Is a Big Shadow

SECOND GRADE
  1 The Scientific Birthday Party
  2 Egbert, What Do You Know About Rain?
  3 Scientists in the Kitchen
  4 Making Dirt
  5 Pop Goes the Corn

THIRD GRADE
  1 Mechanical Toys
  2 Our Place in Space
  3 The Zoo in My Garden
  4 My Special Flashlight

Table 2

Outcomes: Earth & Beyond

LEVELS	EARTH, SKY & PEOPLE	THE CHANGING EARTH	OUR PLACE IN SPACE
1	1.1 Lists ways that the local environment influences daily life.	1.2 Distinguishes major features of the physical environment.	1.3 Identifies features of the day and night sky and relates them to patterns of behaviour in everyday life.
2	2.1 Records ways we monitor and use information about changes to the Earth.	2.2 Describes changes that occur in the local environment.	2.3 Investigates the apparent motion of the sun in relation to the Earth and how this affects everyday life.
3	3.1 Illustrates ways that use of the Earth's resources changes the physical environment.	3.2 Relates changes in the physical environment to physical processes.	3.3 Illustrates patterns of change observable on Earth caused by the relationship between the sun, Earth and moon.
4	4.1 Examines ways scientists investigate the Earth, the solar system and the universe.	4.2 Identifies changes in the atmosphere and the interior of the Earth that cause catastrophic events.	4.3 Locates and describes features of our universe.

Outcomes: Energy & Change

LEVELS	ENERGY & US	TRANSFERRING ENERGY	ENERGY SOURCES & RECEIVERS
1	1.4 Describes ways energy is used in daily life.	1.5 Describes interactions and sequences of connected events.	1.6 Identifies sources of energy in daily life.
2	2.4 Explains ways people in the community use energy.	2.5 Describes properties of light, sound, heating and movement.	2.6 Describes observable changes that occur in two objects that interact, identifying the energy source and receiver.
3	3.4 Reports on patterns of energy use in the home, school and other workplaces.	3.5 Designs and describes ways of enabling or impeding the transfer of energy.	3.6 Identifies the chain of sources and receivers of energy within systems.
4	4.4 Compares energy options available for particular purposes in the community.	4.5 Identifies processes of energy transfer and conditions that affect them.	4.6 Identifies forms and transformations of energy in sequences of interactions.

Outcomes: Life & Living

LEVELS	LIVING TOGETHER	STRUCTURE & FUNCTION	BIODIVERSITY, CHANGE & CONTINUITY
1	1.7 Identifies personal needs and the needs of other familiar living things.	1.8 Identifies observable personal features and those of other familiar living things.	1.9 Identifies personal features and those of animals and plants that change over time.

Table 3: The entire *Science: A Curriculum Profile for Australian Schools* document is available from Heinemann

Outcomes: Life & Living (continued)

LEVELS	LIVING TOGETHER	STRUCTURE & FUNCTION	BIODIVERSITY, CHANGE & CONTINUITY
2	2.7 Describes the types of relationships between living things.	2.8 Links observable features to their functions in familiar living things.	2.9 Compares and contrasts similarities and differences within and between groups of familiar living things.
3	3.7 Maps relationships between living things in a habitat.	3.8 Identifies external and internal features of living things that work together to form systems with particular functions.	3.9 Explains why some living things have become extinct and identifies current endangered species.
4	4.7 Identifies events that affect balance in an ecosystem.	4.8 Explains the functioning of systems within living things.	4.9 Explains how living things have changed over geological time, using evidence from various sources.

Outcomes: Natural & Processed Materials

LEVELS	MATERIALS & THEIR USES	STRUCTURE & PROPERTIES	REACTIONS & CHANGE
1	1.10 Identifies materials and their uses.	1.11 Identifies properties of materials discernible by the senses.	1.12 Identifies changes in materials using the senses.
2	2.10 Lists the ways materials are used for different purposes.	2.11 Describes the substructure of some common materials.	2.12 Distinguishes between changes that cannot be readily reversed and those that can.
3	3.10 Demonstrates how the performance of common materials is altered by combining them with other materials.	3.11 Makes connections between the structure of common materials and their properties.	3.12 Illustrates ways natural materials are processed and the consequences for humans and the environment.
4	4.10 Identifies factors that determine the choice of materials for particular purposes.	4.11 Uses models of the substructure of materials to explain their properties and behaviour.	4.12 Recognises and describes conditions that influence reactions and change in materials.

Outcomes

LEVELS	PLANNING INVESTIGATIONS	CONDUCTING INVESTIGATIONS	PROCESSING DATA
1	1.13 Lists, with support, what is known about familiar situations and suggests questions for investigation.	1.14 Carries out instructions and procedures involving a small number of steps.	1.15 Talks about observations and suggests possible interpretations.
2	2.13 Formulates questions to guide observation and investigations of familiar situations.	2.14 Conducts simple tests and describes observations.	2.15 Identifies patterns and groupings in information to draw conclusions.

Table 3: (continued)

Outcomes *(continued)*

LEVELS	PLANNING INVESTIGATIONS	CONDUCTING INVESTIGATIONS	PROCESSING DATA
3	3.13 Suggests ways of doing investigations, giving consideration to fairness.	3.14 Organises and uses equipment to gather and present information.	3.15 Argues conclusions on the basis of collected information and personal experience.
4	4.13 Identifies factors to be considered in investigations, controls which may be needed, and ways of achieving control.	4.14 Collects and records information accurately as equipment permits and investigation purposes require.	4.15 Draws conclusions linked to the information gathered and the purposes of the investigation.

Outcomes: Working Scientifically

LEVELS	EVALUATING FINDINGS	USING SCIENCE	ACTING RESPONSIBLY
1	1.16 Relates observations and interpretations to other situations.	1.17 Identifies ways science is used in daily life.	1.18 Collaborates with others in the care of living things.
2	2.16 Cooperatively suggests possible improvements to investigations in the light of findings.	2.17 Describes the ways people in the community use science.	2.18 Explains ways that applications of science protect people.
3	3.16 Evaluates the fairness of a test designed and carried out.	3.17 Compares ways of solving problems and finding explanations.	3.18 Identifies ways science is used responsibly in the community.
4	4.16 Reviews the extent to which conclusions are reasonable answers to the	4.17 Describes techniques used to extend the senses.	4.18 Identifies the information needed to make decisions about an application of science.

Scientists in the Kitchen

Children encounter many different materials every day. A drink container, for example, could be made of plastic, plastic-coated paper, glass, ceramic, or metal. They also deal with some things that we and they may not immediately think of as materials, such as air, rocks, plants, and people.

Young children identify properties of materials through their senses. They do not always link properties of materials to their uses—a metal pot for cooking for example—but at the same time they know that a plastic bag is not a suitable container in which to bake something in an oven.

In this unit children reflect on properties of materials and their uses. They explore different types of materials in the kitchen. They identify and describe properties of the materials and relate them to how the materials are used. They examine the substructure of a material and relate that to its properties.

Getting Started

The unit is built around the story of *Wizzy the Whisk Looks for Her Family.*

Materials

- Cardboard cartons and boxes to use as kitchen appliances, cupboards, and drawers.
- Kitchen utensils—whisk, various spoons and forks, beater, ladles, tongs, corkscrew. Some utensils will be made of more than one material (metal and plastic, metal and wood).
- Kitchen containers—pots, pans, bowls, cups, canisters, jars.
- Additional kitchen materials—towels, dish cloths, plastic wrap, aluminum foil.
- Easel, pen, newsprint or flipchart paper.
- Magnifying glasses, sugar, salt, coffee, rice, seeds, flour, jellybeans, fruitcake.
- A cloth bag big enough for children to reach in with both hands.
- Sponge; pot scourer; metal and plastic spoons; plastic, ceramic, metal, and glass cups; dish towel; wooden spoon; beads of different shapes and sizes.
- A collection of refrigerator magnets, a steel plate (e.g., a frying pan) to attract them, and various objects (plastic, wood, glass, metals other than iron and steel) to test whether a magnet sticks to them.

Unit Outline

DAY	WHOLE GROUP ONE	INTRODUCED EXPERIENCES	WHOLE GROUP TWO
1	Tell the story *Wizzy the Whisk Looks for Her Family.* Create a concept map of "What's in my kitchen?" and "What are the things made from?" Have children draw pictures of what is in their kitchen.	Make chocolate crackles (cupcakes made with rice crisps mixed with chocolate). Look at different materials (seeds, rice, flour, jellybeans, sugar) with magnifying glasses.	
2	Look inside the cupboards that were used for the storytelling. Discuss what is in each cupboard and what the items are used for.	Look at fruitcake and decide what is in it! Use magnifying glasses to look at the details of the fruitcake. Draw the fruitcake with all of the substances in it.	Introduce the "Feely Bag." ("Tell me if it feels smooth or rough. Tell me what you think it is made from.")
3	Play kitchen dominoes using actual kitchen utensils.	Have children create a *What is in My Kitchen?* book at home, including drawing and writing (perhaps scribed by adult).	Draw on an easel in response to the question "What sorts of containers would you use to store things in the refrigerator or oven?"
4	Sort and classify materials into metal, plastic, wood, and fabric (signs and items used for group activity). Discuss each group of materials' similarities (look, feel, sound).	Read the *What is in My Kitchen?* books.	Tell a story using kitchen magnets. Ask children to bring in a refrigerator magnet from home.
5	Play musical chairs. As a group, create four categories: plastic, wood, metal, and fabric (signs and items used for group activity).	Sort refrigerator magnets on a metal board (magnets children have brought from home, plus a range of plastic, glass, fabric, metal and wooden magnets).	Tell a story using the different categories of refrigerator magnets (be sure to use some of the children's magnets).
6	Ask children to tell their own stories using the refrigerator magnets. Prepare a group concept map.	Have children make their own magnets (magnetic strip; different materials). Have children write their own stories about the magnets made from different materials.	Invite individual students to read/tell their stories from their books (have them use their magnet).

SUGGESTED AUSTRALIAN SCIENCE PROFILE
OUTCOMES
The unit spans levels 1 and 2 in the strands:

• Natural and Processed Materials (Materials and their uses; Structure and properties)
• Working Scientifically (Conducting investigations; Processing data; Using science)

(Wizzy the kitchen whisk is looking for her family. She looks in all the kitchen cupboards asking, "Are you my Mother or Father?" The replies focus on the material of the object: "I am made of plastic and am round. No, I am not your mother or your father." Wizzy continues until all the items have been discussed and she has found the kitchen whisk family.)

After this, the children explore the properties of materials in the kitchen—foods (seeds, rice, jelly, cake mix) and construction materials (metals, plastics, wood, fabrics)—sorting them, identifying them, reflecting on the ways they are used.

Telling the story
Alicia organized a "home corner" space in her classroom so that the children could sit in it for group time. She made cupboards out of cardboard boxes, with sheets of cardboard as doors that could be opened to reveal the contents. The cupboards contained categories of materials:

A wood cupboard

A plastics cupboard

A pots cupboard

A dish towel drawer

A crockery cupboard

A food cupboard (tins, plastic containers and bags, cardboard packets)

A cutlery drawer

A drawer with plastic wrap, aluminum foil, etc.

A refrigerator (perishables)

Alicia then told her group of young children the story of Wizzy the Whisk—modeled on *Are You My Mother?* by P. D. Eastman (Beginner Books: New York, 1960)—using a cardboard cupboard and kitchen utensils as props. Then she reviewed the story with the children:

ALICIA: Who remembers what is in the first cupboard?
CHILD: Wood.
ALICIA: What have I got here?
CHILD: A wooden spoon.
ALICIA: What would you use a wooden spoon for?
CHILD: Doing cooking.
CHILD   (*motioning round and round with hand*): And boiling.
ALICIA: Everyone look at the next cupboard.
CHILD: Pans.
CHILD: Pots.
ALICIA: Okay, what are the pots and pans made out of?
CHILDREN   (*in chorus*):   Metal.
ALICIA: Is all of the pot made out of metal?
CHILDREN   (*in chorus*):   Yes.
ALICIA   (*pointing to handle*):   What's this bit made out of?
CHILD: That's plastic.
ALICIA: What do you use pots and pans for?
CHILDREN   (*in chorus*):   For cooking.
ALICIA: I have a stove up here. If we put the pots and pans up here on the stove, would they melt if we heated them?
CHILD: No.
CHILD: The plastic would melt if it was there for a long time.
ALICIA: That's why pots and pans are made of metal and not plastic, because the plastic melts if it is on the burner.
CHILD   (*taking pot off the stove*):   It's cooked!

Concept mapping

The children made a group concept map of *materials* (see Figure 1). Alicia encouraged the children to draw their understandings where possible.

Retelling the story

Alicia asked the children to retell the story using the same props she had used. Jan, who is four years old, told this version:

ALICIA: Who remembers how the story started? What was wrong with Wizzy Whisk?

JAN: She was sad because she couldn't find her family.

ALICIA: Yes, she couldn't find her family. Jan, can you help me tell the story? If we forget something, could you other children help us?

JAN: Once upon a time Wizzy Whisk wanted her mother.

ALICIA: And where did she go first?

JAN: She looked in the wood cupboard. (*Opens cupboard. As Wizzy Whisk [high voice]*): Are you my mother? (*As Wooden Spoon [low voice]*): No I'm just wood. (*Closes cupboard*)

Then she went to another cupboard. (*Opens cupboard. As Wizzy Whisk [high voice]*): Are you my mother? *As Pot*): Look, I am made of metal. I can't possibly be your mother.

ALICIA: How was Wizzy the Whisk feeling, Jan?

JAN: She felt sad.

ALICIA: Umm.

JAN: (*moving to cutlery cupboard*): (*As Wizzy Whisk [high voice]*): Are you my mother in there? (*As Fork*): I can't possibly be your mother, I've got forks and metal all over me. I can't possibly be your mother. (*Closes cupboard*)

ALICIA: She must be feeling really sad by now, Jan.

JAN: (*moving to towel cupboard*): Towels and tablecloths. (*As Wizzy Whisk [high voice]*): Are you my mother in there? (*As Dish Towel*): I can't possibly be your mother.

ALICIA: Why wasn't the dish towel—

JAN: (*As Dish Towel*): I'm made out of cotton and I am used to wash dirty dishes. I can't possibly be your mother.

JAN: So she closed up the cupboard. Then she went up to the top [*the utensil rack*].

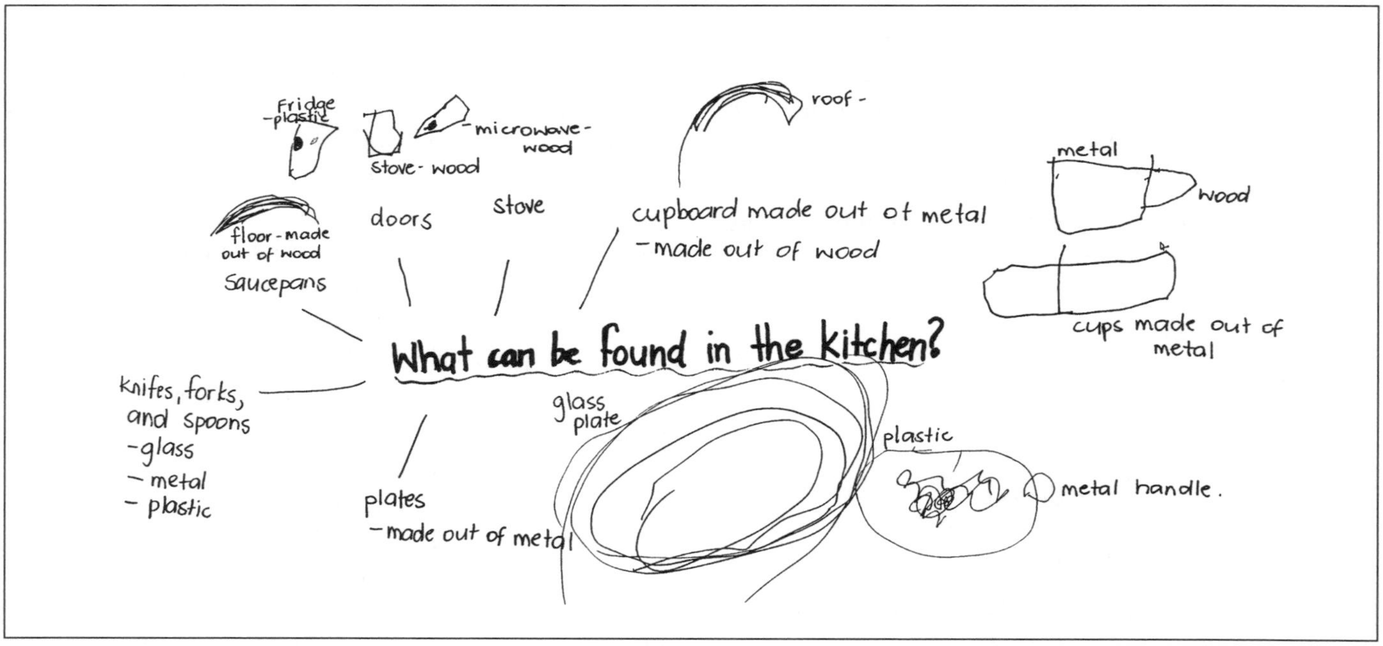

Figure 1: Group concept map

(*As Wizzy Whisk* [*high voice*]): Are you my mother?

(*As Potato Masher*): We've got some metal, do you?

(*As Wizzy Whisk*): Yes, I've got some metal!

(*As Potato Masher*): We've got some plastic, do you?

(*As Wizzy Whisk*): Yes, I've got some plastic.

(*As Potato Masher*): Then you belong.

JAN: Then we will put it up there. (*Places whisk on rack with other utensils*) Wizzy Whisk saw the whole family and lived happily.

Jan's retelling of the story shows a well-developed understanding of materials. It seems more difficult for children to express the reasons for the different uses of a type of material, such as metal.

Activities

The activities below are from the unit outline presented earlier. The comments on the activities are Alicia's.

Make chocolate crackles

By making chocolate crackles, the children experience some of the uses of the different utensils mentioned in the story and come to see that materials have properties that make them suitable for particular purposes. They also begin thinking about what materials are made of—the different substances involved and the substructure of the materials.

Making the chocolate crackles was fun and a great opportunity to consolidate concepts such as what things are made from (for example, the saucepan is metal and plastic), how parts fit together, the ways utensils are used, and whether the materials are solid, liquid, or gas (for example, the chocolate was a solid block and when melted changed state into a liquid).

Use a magnifying glass to look at the substances in materials

Show children a magnifying glass and ask them to look closely at sugar, flour, rice, coffee beans, and other food items that are made up of grains or particles. Let them also look at the chocolate crackles, identifying the different components. The children can draw the details of the granules they see.

The children enjoyed exploring the substances with their fingers and looking at the substances through a magnifying glass. They were not stimulated to draw the detail of what they saw, so I kept this part fairly short, knowing they would pick up the ideas when they looked at fruitcake [see below]. At this stage, they preferred mixing (they used this language) the different substances together and creating their own solids and liquids.

Discover the microworld in a fruitcake

Give children a piece of fruitcake each and ask them to identify the substances in the fruitcake—what is it made of? This builds on the activity with chocolate crackles. The children can separate out some of the components and think about relative quantities. How much cake and how much of each of the different kinds of fruit? How would the fruitcake be different if the quantities were different? They can look at the ingredients with a magnifying glass.

Talk about how materials are often made of combined substances. Make a fruitcake with the children, so they can see how materials combine to give a particular result. This will help them understand that materials have a substructure.

Relate the idea of components to the cooking utensils: a saucepan and its lid are both made of metal; both the lid and the saucepan have handles made of plastic. Encourage children to observe and describe the components and the materials used.

This was quite effective in encouraging children to talk about how materials (the cake) are made up of substances (cherries, raisins, flour, etc.). They also liked thinking about

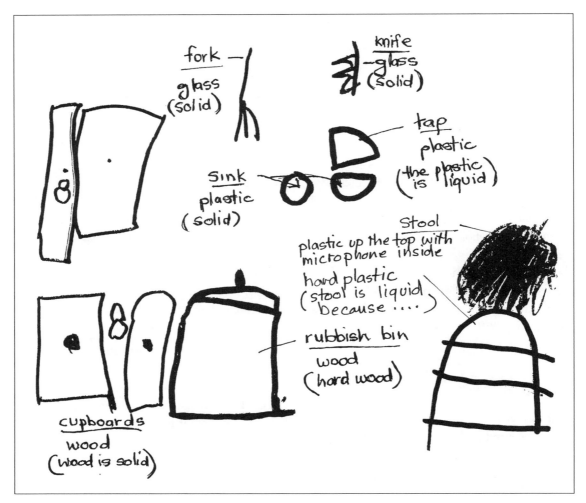

Figure 2: Stephanie's kitchen

the components of different objects around the room and how the objects would be different if the components were different. I'm not sure though that they saw this as the same idea of substructure that we used when we talked about the cake.

Investigate feely bags and feely jars

At the beginning of group time, have the students feel inside a cloth bag that contains different materials. Get them to use terms such as *hard, soft, rough, smooth, round.* Objects could include scouring pads, spoons, plastic lids, metal lids, napkins, sponges, plastic bags, cardboard beads. Make feely jars with some similar and some contrasting materials—water, milk; flour, salt; sugar,

powdered sugar; honey, maple syrup. Children can describe, distinguish, and compare the properties of these materials.

These bags and jars stimulate the ideas of substructure and microworlds hidden from direct view—an important idea in science.

Play kitchen dominoes

Play a game of group dominoes with kitchen utensils. Start the game by placing one object on the floor (the kitchen whisk used in the story, for example). Children add either something metal to the whisk end or something plastic to the handle end. Include in the collection some items made of one material only, the majority made of two or three materials, so that changes in material occur regularly throughout the game. Talk

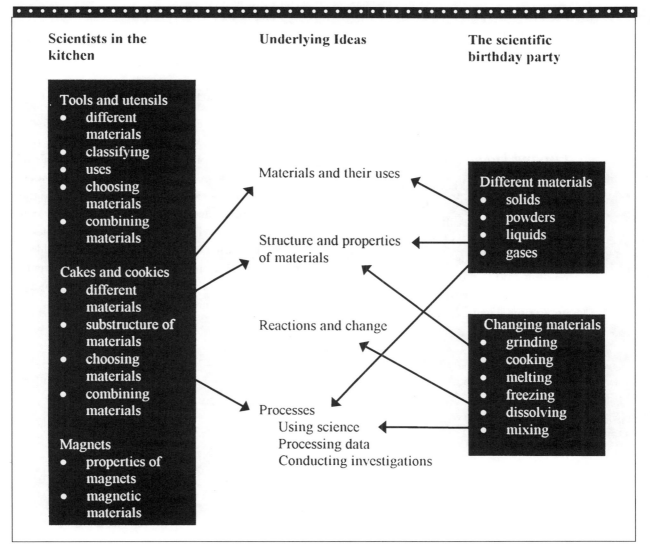

Figure 3: Link chart

with the children about why particular materials are used in the utensils and look for patterns in the choices—for example, handles are usually made from plastic or wood; blades (in beaters, whisks, knives) are made from metal.

This activity was simple to organize and interested all the children. I wanted them to think about the different materials that one object can be made from and the different uses of a particular material. The group concept map gave me a good starting point for selecting the materials. Because I used objects from around the room as well as the objects I had used in

the storytelling, the activity related well to the children's everyday experiences.

Play musical kitchen utensils
Organize a game of musical kitchen utensils to the tune of *The March of the Wooden Soldiers*. Give each child a utensil—a wooden spoon, metal pot or plastic cup. (Alternatively, give them pictures of utensils, which they hold or pin to their shirts.) Discuss the material each object is made of.

Place chairs in spaces identified as parts of the kitchen, like cupboards and drawers, where materials are grouped. A chalk line around clusters of chairs works well. When the music stops, children run to sit in the area that their utensil is likely to be found.

Play the music and remove chairs as required. With younger children you may not need to remove a chair—simply giving them a new utensil creates enough variety and motivation.

Linking Home and School

Alicia made small booklets for each child to take home. The booklets encouraged the children to locate different materials in their kitchen at home and draw pictures of them. The children brought their booklets back for reading and discussion, either individually with Alicia or with the other children at group time. Figure 2 is a page from Stephanie's booklet.

Link to Another Unit

This unit links readily to "The Scientific Birthday Party" (see Figure 3).

ALICIA'S REFLECTIONS ON THE UNIT

This unit emphasizes storytelling and the children's home experiences in the kitchen as a fruitful and effective starting point for talking about materials, properties, and uses.

All the elements of the unit related to the children's everyday experiences and as a result I felt the children were motivated to learn about what materials are made from. Children learned scientific concepts in a fun and stimulating way through experiences such as storytelling, games, and cooking.

Cycles of Life

"Tadpole to frog" is a life cycle commonly taught to young children. Tadpoles are readily accessible (in the right season), and children enjoy them. The transformation of a tadpole to a frog is fascinating in itself. It is also a wonderful springboard to thinking about life cycles and concepts like living, growing, and stages of life.

This unit integrates the study of life cycles with language development. It extends the theme beyond frogs to other animals and plants, so that children see life cycles as a universal aspect of living things, one to which their own life and growth relate.

Two approaches to the unit are presented in the following table. One suited to pre-schoolers (Sandra's group), the other to second and/or third graders (Nick's group). The latter goes some distance toward the extensions suggested above.

Sandra's Approach to the Unit

Getting started:
Life and growth

Beginnings and ends, but what is in between?
Sandra showed pictures and a film strip and asked the children to describe how their bodies have changed since they were born and what will happen as they grow older. Then she asked about what happens to various animals and plants as they grow.

Many children had scientific views about what something started as, and what it grew to, but they were often unclear about the changes that took place in between. Figure 1 is Maryann's explanation of how carrots grow.

Materials

- Books and references on tadpoles, frogs, and other life cycles (including humans).
- Materials for making books (including computers).
- Cards on which children can draw life-stage pictures to be put in sequence.
- Photographs and drawings of humans at different ages.

STEP	SANDRA'S GROUP (PRESCHOOL)	NICK'S GROUP (2ND/3RD GRADE)
Getting started	Draw pictures showing how humans and other animals and plants change as they grow older.	Draw pictures showing how humans and other animals and plants change as they grow older. Write about these drawings. Produce a concept map on life cycles.
Tadpoles and frogs	Work with a number of factual texts. Construct a text of your own. Go out looking for frogs and tadpoles. Search out new information, then revise and extend the text. Have children take home copies of their own text to read with parents and caregivers.	Write down what the class knows and what they want to find out about the frog life cycle. Discuss ideas in small groups and large groups. Read a factual text on the frog life cycle. Have children assemble fact sheets based on their own knowledge and texts. These lead eventually to a class "Frog Fact Book." Ask the children to share new words they have found, play word-association games. Go out looking for frogs and tadpoles. Working in small groups and with the help of a computer, write books on the frog's life cycle.
Other life cycles		Try to apply the idea of a life cycle to other animals and plants, drawing pictures, sequencing cards, using books.
A closer look at humans	Ask children to bring photographs of themselves and their families, putting them in order from young to old.	Analyze photographs and drawings, seeing how shapes and proportions change as people get older. Draw a life cycle for humans.

Table 1: Cycles of life

Figure 1: Maryann explains how carrots grow

Tadpoles and frogs

What do the students already know about frogs and their life cycle?

Children talked about their experiences with frogs, where frogs are found, and how they change as they grow.

Presenting the life cycle

The children didn't have the scientific language of the frog cycle. I gave it to them, with the help of a series of pictures (see Figure 2) and a factual text that contained the language I was using.

Early in the teaching sequence, we worked together to construct a cyclic picture of what we knew about the frog life cycle (see Figure 3)25

. Students' personal interaction—with each other and with me—is important. I use it as a way to challenge the children's ideas and build their language.

Using texts and creating texts

The children used a variety of texts—fact and fiction, big books and small. They went on to produce texts of their own.

They dictated their own texts, jointly constructed with me, as they accumulated more knowledge about the topic. Their texts were able to show them their own learning, and demonstrate that it can be recorded and that they can communicate in writing to other people.

Our first attempt (Figure 4) was a reconstruction of the text we had been using. The next attempt was more extensive. Finally, we made a book that each child took home.

Taking their books home gave a point to their writing: they recorded what they wanted to say and communicated it to a chosen audience.

The students' final version is shown in Figure 5.

Field trips

The language and science combination is greatly strengthened by watching and listening to frogs and tadpoles in the places they live. The time of year needs to be right for tadpoles, but frogs can be found any time. Sandra's children visited a local river. It was wonderfully stimulating for them, encouraging them to talk about their experience and relate it to what they had seen earlier in texts.

A closer look at humans

Life cycles are a universal phenomenon that apply to all living things. Sandra did not want to give her students the impression

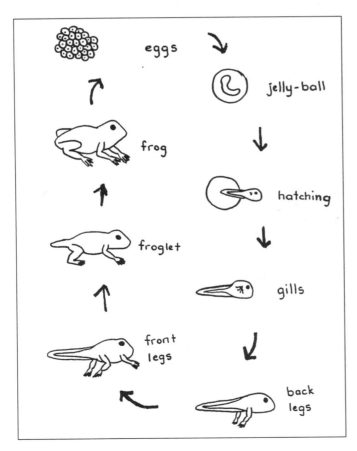

Figure 2: Frog life cycle

Unit Outline

GETTING STARTED: LIFE AND GROWTH
• Discuss how particular living things begin, grow, and change.
• Tadpoles and frogs (a language approach)
• Find out what students know about frogs and their life cycle.
• Read and write about the frog's life cycle.
• Observe frogs firsthand.
• Write a class book on frogs and their life cycle.

OTHER LIFE CYCLES
• Read and write about life cycles and development stages in other animals and plants.

A CLOSER LOOK AT HUMANS
• Study the stages in human development, relating them to the students and people they know.

SUGGESTED AUSTRALIAN SCIENCE PROFILE OUTCOMES
The unit spans levels 1 and 2 in the strands:

• Life and Living (Biodiversity, change, and continuity; Structure and function)
• Working Scientifically (Planning investigations; Conducting investigations; Processing data; Evaluating findings)

EXTENDING THE UNIT
The unit could readily be extended to a broader study of frogs and their habitats, to include:

• Level 3 in Biodiversity, change and continuity
• Levels 1, 2, and 3 in Living together
• Levels 1, 2, and 3 in Acting responsibly

Frogs are sensitive to environmental change, and many species are endangered. Extending the unit to frogs in their habitats adds a new theme that fits well with life cycles and the language approach of the unit as written.

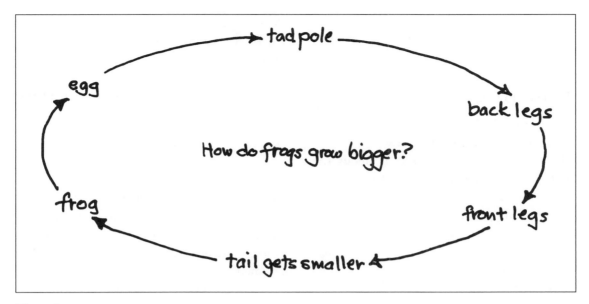

Figure 3

Frogs are amphibians. They start inside jelly balls. When they hatch out they are tadpoles. They can breathe under water. Soon they grow their back legs and then they grow their front legs. The tail gets shorter and they turn into frogs. The frog gets bigger and it breathes out of the water. It starts all over again.

Figure 4: The students' first version of the text

that frogs are the only things that have a life cycle. Most of all, the children needed to include themselves—human beings—into the whole picture. Children are fascinated by the human life cycle, and stimulated to ask all kinds of questions about themselves and their bodies—another unit of work!

The children brought photographs of themselves and others in their families—babies, parents, uncles, grandparents. Children who couldn't bring photographs cut pictures from magazines.

They first arranged their photos in order individually. Then, in small groups, they combined photos and made longer sequences, which they examined for changes. They talked about the sorts of

things people do at different stages of their lives. They enjoyed both the way things change and the way they stay the same: "Your head, ears, nose and mouth all get bigger as you grow up." "Everything I have got, I was born with as a baby."

Not many of Sandra's group alluded to death. They talked about death in relation to insects, plants, and animals, but rarely about death and people. Only one child commented: "My Dad's mom died. It's sad." Sandra concluded the unit with stories that depicted lifetimes—beginnings and endings and new lives.

Nick's Approach to the Unit

Getting Started:
Life and growth

In Nick's group, all the children had clear ideas about what would happen as they grew older "We will get bigger, grow old, and then die." Nick asked about cats and birds and dinosaurs, then carrots and apples. After some discussion, the children drew pictures of a plant or animal showing "Where it came from" and "What it grows to."

Then the children wrote about their

life cycle drawings (see Figures 6 and 7). Their writing reveals a wide range of literacy levels.

Tadpoles to frogs

Recording what students know and want to find out about frog life cycles

The children wrote down facts about the frog life cycle that they thought they really knew and ones they would like to find out. These notations revealed their knowledge, interests, and language. Nick observed: "I want the children to extend their language from a common sense perspective to a more scientific one. This doesn't just happen: you have to plan for it."

Frogs are amphibians. They jump in the water and on the land. They can swim.

The mother frog lays hundreds of eggs in the water, or ditches. The daddy frog puts liquid on the eggs. The mom and dad frog swim away. The eggs sink to the bottom and then back up where it is warm.

The egg is inside the jelly ball. The egg changes shape into a tadpole. After ten days the tadpoles are ready to come out.

The tadpoles have wriggled out. They swim away. Each tadpole has gills to breathe. The tadpole swims with its tail. The tail wriggles.

The tadpole grows back legs. It takes five weeks. The gills have gone into the tadpole's body. They turn into lungs and the tadpole breathes using the lungs. It breathes air.

After ten weeks the front legs have grown. They need to swim to find food. They eat tiny plants and grass in the water.

It is a froglet. It starts to live on the land and it has got a shorter tail. It has nearly turned into a frog.

After fifteen weeks it has turned into a frog. It lives on the land and ribbits and jumps. It still goes back into the water. It lays eggs and the life cycle happens all over again.

Figure 5: The final version of the text

Constructing a concept map

With their answers to what they knew and what they wanted to find out as a basis, Nick and the children put together a concept map. They talked about why they linked the ideas they linked. Often the children seemed to have ideas about what happens but were limited by their language.

Group discussions

Throughout the unit, there were many discussions, often in small groups, sometimes as a class. The children were comfortable in these discussions, using language that seemed suitable to them. Their comments show them beginning to use scientific language:

"It's a life cycle because it goes round and round."

"They start off as eggs then they change into different forms, then it starts all over again."

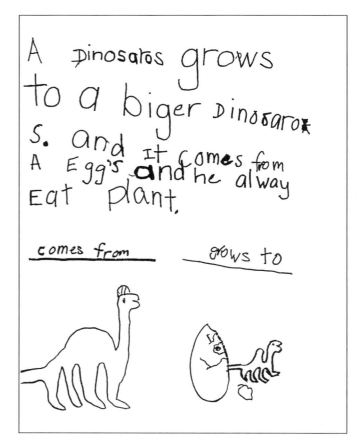

Figure 6: Max writes about his dinosaur

"If we didn't have a female in our life cycle we couldn't start again."

"They move around in their eggs. If they didn't move they wouldn't be able to get out."

"They change shape in their eggs."

"The tadpoles swim out of the eggs in different directions by wriggling their tails."

"The tail gets bigger then later it gets shorter."

"As the tadpole grows the tail doesn't get thinner. It just looks like that because its body gets bigger."

"Even after the tail drops off and it's a frog you can still see a little bit of its tail."

The word *cycle* was a problem for some children: they had encountered it in a number of contexts—a bike, to ride a bike, to go round and round, to change from one thing to another and back, etc. Yet life cycles are none of these: life does not really go round and round. The frog that is born is not the one that died. It is the pattern of life and death that scientists call a *cycle*. Often in science common words are given uncommon meanings.

Reading and book research

As a lead-in to the students' book research on frogs, Nick read a factual account of the frog life cycle. This gave the children a framework for asking questions and for identifying relevant information in their own research.

Using text and writing fact sheets

During their research, the children kept their own fact sheets (see Figure 8). Children recorded not only information about the life cycle, but about frogs generally.

Word associations

As a way of summarizing progress with their research, the children in groups listed as many words as they knew or could find about particular subtopics, such as skin (camouflage, colorful, patterns, smooth, shiny, lumpy, warty, stripes, spots, wet) and voices (croaky, mating call, useful, ribbit,

Figure 7: Rebecca writes about her apple seed

Figure 8: Tara's fact sheets

loud, echoes, sound, like crickets, puff cheeks).

Field trips

The class went to a botanical garden, where they looked for frogs, connected their earlier reading and discussion to what they saw, made size and pattern estimations, and matched frog features they had read about with actual specimens. They ex-

perienced the sights and smells of the frogs' environment and followed up by reading about the effects of environmental change on frogs. All of these experiences were well suited to writing, poetry, storytelling and drama.

Producing the "Frog Fact Book"

Toward the end of the segment the children composed a class "Frog Fact Book." Based on

The male frog has to mate with the female first.

The female frog lays her eggs in warmish water in springtime. Then the female frog leaves her eggs. They sink to the bottom then come back up.

The eggs are like little black dots in jelly stuff. The eggs change their shape and look like black jelly beans. While they are in the jelly the eggs eat some of the jelly.

After about ten days they are tadpoles and they wriggle out of the eggs. When they are just born they have very small mouths. As they get bigger their mouths get bigger too. They can only eat tiny bits of food.

When they are tadpoles they breathe with their gills. When they are tadpoles they eat plankton, little dead fish, other tadpoles, and plants. Dragon flies, water scorpions, birds and other tadpoles eat them.

It takes about 12 weeks to turn into a frog. After six weeks they get their back legs and after that they get their front legs. Then the tail goes back into its body. Its legs get bigger and the whole body gets bigger. Their lungs grow so they can breathe on land.

The frogs have to go in water because they might get dried up and die.

Frogs are amphibians and cold blooded. They have a long sticky tongue so they can catch insects. Their voice pattern attracts the female. When they call their throats puff up. Frogs call to their own kind.

Frogs have long back legs to jump and different frogs can jump different distances. They use their front legs to push the water away as they swim and their back legs are used to kick.

There are lots of different kinds of frogs. The tree frog has sucker pads to help it climb. Desert frogs lay flat on the ground to get water through their skin.

Frogs eat moving things. Sometimes they can mistake a falling leaf for an insect. Some frogs eat other frogs.

They lay their eggs and start all over again.

Figure 9: **The text of the "Fact Frog Book"**

their fact sheets, it went beyond the life cycle. The complete text of the children's book is included in Figure 9.

Small-group book production, using computers

Children in pairs and trios prepared their own texts on the frog's life cycle. They wrote rough drafts in longhand, entered them onto the computer, and made final adjustments using the word processor. Michelle and Sandra's first draft is shown in Figure 10. Once the text was complete, the children added illustrations and headings, again using the computer.

Other life cycles

Nick's children also needed to appreciate that all living things have life cycles and to place themselves and frogs into the larger schema.

Using books

Nick had begun the unit by asking the children to draw and write about something in their environment that changes as it grows. He returned to those pictures now. The children used texts to follow up on their earlier ideas, find out about other life cycles, and compare them with the frog's.

Making puzzles

The children made puzzles by putting parts of various life cycles on cards and asking other students to put the cards in sequence.

They compared cycles and stages of growth for different living things and discussed how and why living things change.

They found the metamorphosis of the butterfly difficult even though they had in Spring the female frog lays the eggs it lays it in the water and the frogs leave the eggs untill they Hatchs the tadpole has gills to breffh trouth when it turns into a froglet it grows & lungs. when it is a frog it lives on land it jumps from place to place tadpoles can't Do that So they have to live on the water it eats fish and plants and the female lays its eggs on top of the male and theye are all kind of frogs. and frogs call thier own kind of frogs. the male mates with the female first and tad poles have small mouths and eyes. you can't See thier mouth and nose.

uk uk uk uk uk

icrick

Figure 10: **Michelle and Sandra's draft**

A closer look at humans

studied the transition of tadpole to frog. "To them it is some magical process, so hard to comprehend, yet they can cope and remember so well all sorts of fascinating and unusual facts."

The children collected photographs of themselves and others in their families as well as drawings and pictures from magazines. They found out the heights of people at different ages. They compared body proportions for babies, young children, teenagers, young adults, and old people, looking at changes in shape and changes in body size compared to head size. The children made silhouettes and asked other children to predict the age of the person depicted. Finally, the children used books to find out about the life cycle of humans and showed it in sequences of drawings.

The Dark
Is a Big Shadow

From a young age, children are aware of the rhythm of day and night. Eventually many take it for granted, a comfortable routine. This unit helps children reflect on the patterns of day and night and leads them toward the idea that the Earth spins. This amazing idea is not easy to grasp or to demonstrate! The unit helps children think in terms of models to explain what they see, as part of working scientifically. They expand their understanding of day and night and their place in space, developing concepts such as time, position, shadow, light, movement, planets, sky. They also learn more about living things by considering the effects of night and day on plants and animals.

Beginning: Day and Night, Light and Dark

The sky by day

The children went into the playground to observe and discuss things they could see in the sky: the sun, clouds, a bird flying. What are some of the things the sun gives us? What happens in the shadows? They talked about light and warmth, and tested their ideas, standing in the shadows and then in full sunlight. Back in the classroom, we discussed ideas and made a summary.

What happens at night?

The children knew that the sun couldn't be seen at night, and that the night was dark and cold compared with the day. They talked about living at night—in their houses and, for some of them, when they go camping. What do they do? What do they see? Are there birds or animals around? What do plants do? What is in the sky? They drew pictures to explain what it is like at night.

Materials

- Drapes or window covering for blackout.
- Big cartons that children can hop into and close.
- Books and posters about nocturnal animals.
- Flashlights (and batteries).
- Balls of different sizes.
- A world globe and little figures made of modeling clay that can be stuck onto the globe.
- Materials to make shadow puppets.
- Mirrors.

Unit Outline

BEGINNING: DAY AND NIGHT, LIGHT AND DARK
- The sky by day
- What happens at night?
- Living in the dark
- Putting it together: comparing day and night

WHAT HAPPENS TO THE SUN AT NIGHT?
- Children's ideas
- Modeling: playing with spheres and shadows

NIGHT AND DAY BOOKS: OBSERVATIONS, QUESTIONS, AND IDEAS
- Involving parents
- Using the Night and Day books

EXPLORING SHADOWS—OF HUMANS, STICKS, AND OTHER THINGS
- Orientation
- Shadows from flashlights
- Shadows from the sun
- Me and my shadow
- A working definition of a shadow
- The apparent motion of the sun

MODELS OF NIGHT AND DAY
- Children's views
- Which model is "right"?
- Demonstrating the model

CONSOLIDATING LEARNING

SUGGESTED AUSTRALIAN SCIENCE PROFILE OUTCOMES
This unit spans levels 1 and 2 in the strands:

- Earth and Beyond (Our place in space)
- Working Scientifically (Planning investigations; Conducting investigations; Processing data; Evaluating findings)

Living in the dark

We simulated darkness in the classroom: children sat in groups of four in big cartons that we could close. They had flashlights, but for part of the time at least, they sat very still in the dark. What did they feel? Their eyes became accustomed to the dark. They listened more carefully for sounds around them. We discussed different responses to the dark; it can be frightening not to know what is going on around you. We considered how to act responsibly in the dark—wearing bright clothes when walking, for example.

We made a list of people who work at night, in factories and hospitals, on the radio, in clubs, policemen, taxi drivers, truck drivers. We also listed animals that come out at night, like possums, mice, rabbits, and owls. Only a few of the children had actually seen these animals. We looked at books with photos and read about the activities of nocturnal animals. The children drew pictures about living in the dark.

Putting it together: comparing day and night

We focused on two aspects:

- the rhythm of day and night—the sorts of things people do at different times, and the idea that the clock is linked to the passing of day and night. The children told about their daily routine.
- a comparison of the features of day and night.

The class made two lists, one of features of day, and the other of night. From the lists they identified pairs of ideas, such as stars/no stars, sun/no sun, and so on.

What Happens to the Sun at Night?

Children's ideas

We asked, What causes day to change to night? What happens to the sun at night? The children worked individually, drawing pictures and explaining them (see Figure 1). Where necessary, we scribed for them. The children's pictures not only gave us information about their understanding of day and

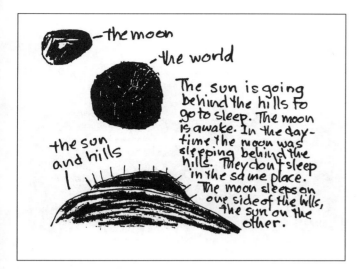

Figure 1: Tegan's ideas about day and night

night, but also show the shapes used to depict the world, the sun, and the moon. We mounted the pictures on the classroom wall.

Some common explanations were:

- At night the sun hides behind clouds.
- At night the sun hides behind mountains.
- The earth spins around and one side is bright and one dark.

Some children drew a spinning Earth, but did not use this idea in their explanation.

Modeling: playing with spheres and shadows

Nearly all the children saw the Earth as a sphere. We talked about the idea of the Earth being like a ball, and gave them flashlights and different-size balls to tinker with. Groups took turns inside the dark cartons and described what they saw as they shone the flashlights on the different balls.

Night and Day Books

Throughout the unit the children made observations and recorded them in their *Night and Day* books (see Figure 2). Does sunrise occur at the same time on successive days? Does it rise from the same place? Are birds to be seen at night? Does the moon ever go behind a cloud without causing day, or the sun without causing night? Are the sun and the moon ever out together?

Involving parents

For observations outside of school, we enlisted the help of parents and caregivers. You can use the sample letter in Figure 3, or the suggested introduction to the *Night and Day* book in Figure 4. The children needed help in writing down what they saw and someone to share their activities with—a sunrise is more enjoyable when you see it with someone else.

We encouraged parents to ask the children for explanations, but to resist giving the children "right answers" at this stage. We wanted children to build up their observations and questions before confronting the idea that the Earth is spinning.

Using the Night and Day books

Children shared their findings in regular reporting sessions, partly to use the information and partly to affirm the worth of the activity and experience. Often these sessions suggested things that all children could look at and we could discuss a couple of days later. The children took pride in their books, and enjoyed the home activities.

They often asked questions we did not wish to pursue at this stage (about particular stars or artificial satellites, for example). We tried to maintain our focus on ideas of night and day by redirecting these questions after answering them briefly ("Do you think the satellites are still there in the day time?"). We also made available a collection of reference books and, with older classes, CD-ROM resources, which children used at various times to answer their questions.

We found that our choice of words was very important. For example, asking the children, Where does the sun go at night? drew quite different responses from, What happens to the sun at night? Much of our everyday language about day and night implies a certain understanding (The sun is going down. The

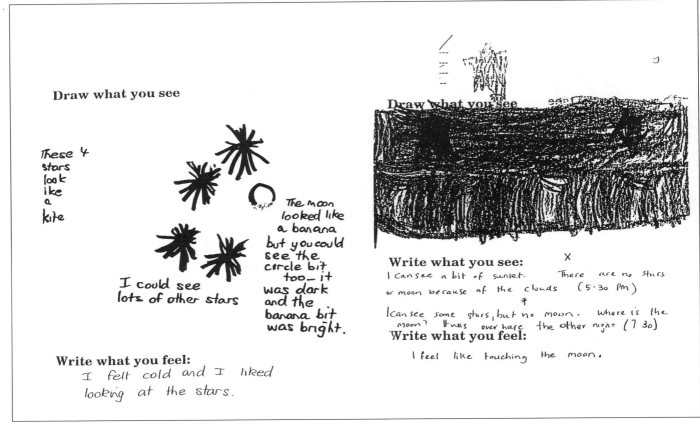

Draw what you see

These 4 stars look like a kite

I could see lots of other stars

The moon looked like a banana but you could see the circle bit too— it was dark and the banana bit was bright.

Write what you feel:
I felt cold and I liked looking at the stars.

Draw what you see

Write what you see: X
I can see a bit of sunset. There are no stars or moon because of the clouds (5.30 PM)

    *

I can see some stars, but no moon. Where is the moon? It was over here the other night (7.30)

Write what you feel:
I feel like touching the moon.

Figure 2: The Night and Day book consisted of . . .

stars are coming out.). Scientific views contrast with common language! Similarly, some children used *world* instead of *Earth*, and thought of earth only as soil. We allowed either word and kept a world globe on display.

Exploring Shadows— of Humans, Sticks and Other Things

For children to think of nighttime as being a shadow, they need to understand that the Earth is a sphere (or at least a finite object) and how light from the sun causes shadows.

Most children do not understand shadows very well, partly because we use the word in different ways—sometimes the shape cast on the ground beyond an object, sometimes the dark side of an object. To suggest the movement of the sun, the shadow cast on the ground is helpful, but with day

and night, it is the sense of the dark side, or "standing in the shadow," that is important.

A suitable working definition of a shadow is a place where light has been blocked from going.

Orientation
The children talked about their experiences in the darkened box and with balls and flashlights. What was it like? What did they see? They talked about shadows. What caused shadows? Where else do we find shadows? Their ideas provided a springboard for the indoor activities with flashlights and overhead projectors and the sunlight activities outdoors.

Shadows from flashlights
The children completed activities to establish that a shadow is formed when light has been blocked by some object:

Dear Parents,

In science, we are just starting a *Night and Day* unit in which your child will learn about changes that occur in between day and night, shadows, and the movements of the sun and moon. An important part of the unit is for children to notice things in the sky: what difference does it make when the sun or the moon goes behind a cloud? do birds make as much noise at sunset as they do at sunrise? does the sun rise at the same time every morning? in the same place?

I invite you to be part of the unit by helping your child make these observations and record them in his or her *Night and Day* book. Your help is particularly important at night and in the early morning, when I can't be there! Your child can draw and write in the book. Sometimes you might like to write for your child, putting down what he or she tells you. We will also use the "Night and Day" Book at school to record observations in the daytime.

By all means ask what your child thinks is happening and why (and help him or her write down these ideas), but hold back at this stage from giving the "right answers." The students will build up information and ideas over the next few weeks, and then we will work together to interpret that information.

I would like to thank you very much for your assistance and cooperation. I hope you and your child make some interesting observations together and have an enjoyable time.

Yours sincerely,

Figure 3: A suggested letter home

- Making and using shadow puppets.
- Moving the light source rather than the puppets.
- Shining flashlights on sticks (e.g., pencils stuck in a clay base), balls, chairs, and other objects (see Figure 5).

Shadows from the sun

Children became aware of the apparent regular movement of the sun across the sky and the relationships between the sun's direction and shadows by drawing around their shadows, looking at the shadows' of buildings, trees, dogs, sticks, etc., predicting shadows (for themselves and other objects), and plotting how shadows change with time (see Figure 6).

Me and my shadow

Children explored their own shadows: can they make it thin? make it short?

Can they "disconnect" their shadows from their bodies? Do their shadows really

Your child's *Night and Day* book is for her or him to note their observations of the sky and things that happen by night and by day.

Please help with these observations and the recording process. It would be great if you could do this a number of times over the next two weeks. Some suggestions:

- watch sunrise and a sunset.
- observe something twice on one night to see how things change (e.g., how the moon changes position).
- look at the same thing on different nights to see what is the same and what is different.
- look for animals and birds, what they are doing, and whether this differs during the day and during the night.
- look at clouds and the ways they move (is the moon moving fast, or is it the clouds that are moving?).
- how does it feel, out in the open before dawn, waiting for the sun to rise: what do you hear? what can you see?

If you have binoculars, looking at clouds, the moon, and the stars can be fun. Don't attempt to look at the sun, especially not through binoculars: you will burn your eyes, just as the sun shining through a magnifying glass burns paper.

Help your child draw pictures and write down what he or she sees and feels. You can perhaps write down what he or she tells you to.

Help your child notice things he or she might otherwise miss. For example, the moon can be high in the sky even after sunrise, and the sun goes down in the same place (e.g., behind the same tree) on successive nights. Ask your child for explanations and help write down these ideas. Resist the temptation to give the "right answers" at this stage: we will come to those later, in school.

Thanks for your help. Have an enjoyable time.

Figure 4: Introduction to Night and Day book

Figure 5: Shadows from flashlights

follow them everywhere? How can they lose their shadows?

Many children used the term reflection to describe a shadow. We introduced mirrors during the shadow activities so children could compare the two. Shadows do not show facial features or the color of hair; shadows can drape across a chair, or be partly on the ground and partly up a wall. A reflection is always "in the mirror"; the shadow is always "away from the light."

A working definition of a shadow

The whole class developed a concept map on shadows and, from that, talked about a working definition of a shadow, along the lines that blocking light gives rise to a shadow. Then children wrote their own definitions (sometimes with help from us in scribing them).

The apparent movement of the sun

Drawing from the work with shadows and our observations of sunrise, sunset, and the daily movement of the sun, we agreed as a group that the sun apparently moved from east to west across the sky and that it rose and set at about the same time on successive days. We underlined the idea that the sun casts shadows. Standing in a shadow, sunlight is blocked. The shadow is dark and cold, and you can't see the sun.

Models of Night and Day

Children's views

In groups of four, children experimented with a sphere (the Earth) that had a day figure stuck to it (a person) and a flashlight (the sun) to propose explanations of night and

At 10 o'clock the shadow was big. It got smaller at 12 o'clock and at 3 o'clock it got big again.

Figure 6: **Shadows move during the day**

day. Each group presented their explanation to the class. Three explanations emerged:

- The sun goes around the Earth shining on it and lighting up different parts. The Earth is stationary.
- The sun turns around and the Earth is stationary. This causes night and day, assuming the sun shines in one direction, like the flashlight.
- The Earth spins around and the sun shines on it causing night on one side and day on the other.

Which model is "right"?
The children decided that all the models were interesting and could explain night and day. How could they choose which one was "right"?

We noted that up until about three hundred years ago humans had preferred the first model, that the sun went around the Earth. People had argued against the second model, because they felt the sun probably shone in all directions, more like a light

bulb or campfire than a flashlight. Scientists now believe the third model, that the Earth spins around on itself, and have been able to do experiments which show that the Earth spins.

Vivien commented how difficult this was for her to believe because she could not feel the Earth turning the way she could a merry-go-round. Thus she recognized how implausible this probably seemed to the children and promoted the idea that science speaks from experiment and experience, not simply authority.

Demonstrating the model
We introduced a world globe and modeled the spin of the Earth to small groups in turn so we could engage them in close discussion. We set a little clay person on Australia and light coming from an overhead projector. The children watched the "person's" shadow changing and linked it to their own observations in the playground.

Children saw the shadow side of Earth, and how the little person went into it and

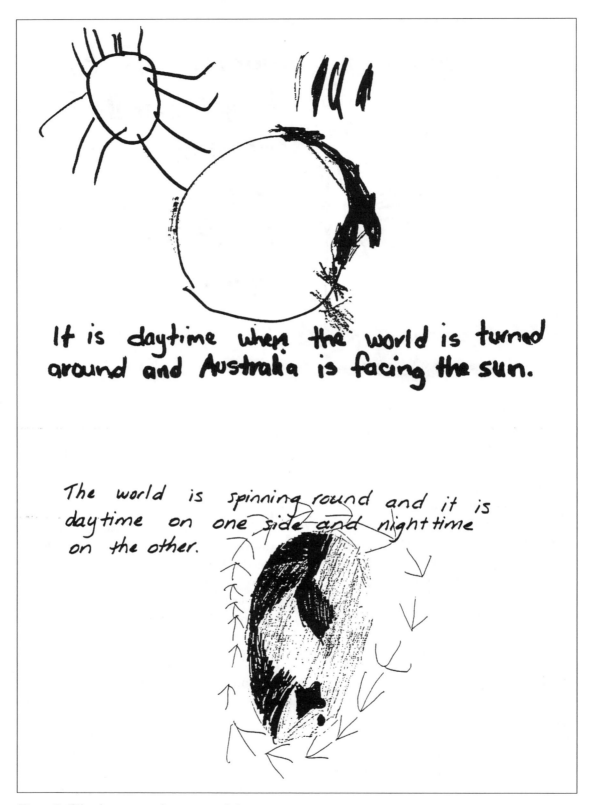

It is daytime when the world is turned around and Australia is facing the sun.

The world is spinning round and it is daytime on one side and night time on the other.

Figure 7: What happens to the sun at night?

out of it, spending half of the time in the dark and half in the light. They tried looking from the dark side and realized they could not see the "sun" from there. Night was like a big shadow made by the Earth itself!

Children who had been overseas or had friends overseas were interested in those places on the globe. We talked about whether those countries would be experiencing day or night when it was day in Australia, and used the model to work it out.

Consolidating Learning

The class read the big book *The Sun Is Always Shining Somewhere* (A. Fowler, Children's Press, Chicago, 1991), which addresses many of the concepts covered in this unit.

Children reviewed their *Night and Day* books. We looked for observations in them that suggested the Earth was spinning—things like the moon and stars also moving

from east to west—and addressed any outstanding questions the children had.

Finally, the children drew pictures explaining how they thought night and day happened, in answer to the question "What happens to the sun at night?" Two examples are shown in Figure 7.

Final Reflections

The unit was a challenge for the children, since they had to work with large-scale phenomena like the sun and Earth and model them with little balls and flashlight beams. Children achieved different levels of awareness of day and night, shadows, and behavior and time; many were able to clearly use the idea of the spinning Earth. As they continue their learning in science, their understanding will be extended to the moon, the planets, and more distant features of our wonderful universe.

If the Cow Runs Out of Grass, She Stops

So much of our lives and the things we do depend on energy. Children already have a feeling for that, even though they probably haven't really thought of it in terms of energy.

This unit helps children build a concept of energy by focusing not on what energy *is*, but what happens if it *runs out*:

What happens if the mower runs out of gas?

What happens if the fire runs out of wood?

What happens if the cow runs out of grass?

The answer is always the same: it stops. The children keep building and generalizing about what energy is.

This is a game the children can play too, asking questions of each other, using the teacher's examples to guide them. It is a lateral-thinking game, just right for inventing ridiculous situations and drawing cartoons to illustrate them.

For all its humor, the game leads to some serious questions: there *are* people running out of food; the world *is* running out of some types of fuel. The children can offer some possible answers—sharing, conserving, recycling, inventing.

Getting Started: What if. . . ?

Chris asked the children a series of questions, like What if the mower ran out of gas? that focused on the idea of things stopping. He guided them to three kinds of energy:

- Energy to make things move—a car, a dog, a clock, a toy, a flag in the wind. (He slipped in the word energy for some examples: What would happen if the dancer ran out of energy?)
- Energy to make things hot—fires and lights.
- Energy to make things—especially plants and animals, but also

Materials

- Drawing materials.
- Material for making big books.
- Books/posters/films about shortages of food and energy locally or around the world.

Unit Outline

- Getting started: What if . . .
- Making a big book
- Talking about energy: what does energy do?
- Field Trip: What if the baker's electricity went off?
- Film and books: Some people are running out of fuel
- Toward solutions: What can be done to help?
- Bringing it together: Making a little book

SUGGESTED AUSTRALIAN SCIENCE PROFILE OUTCOMES:
The unit spans levels 1 and 2 in the strands:

- Energy and Change (Energy and us; Energy sources and receivers)
- Working Scientifically (Using science; Acting responsibly)

EXTENDING THE UNIT
The unit could readily be extended to include level 3 by looking into more detailed patterns of energy use and conservation in the home community and by considering various energy sources and ways to control energy waste. Alternatively, the unit could be the springboard for "sideways extensions" into particular phenomena in everyday life (sound, collisions, magnets, and so on), adding more hands-on experiences.

manufactured products. (Chris again used the word energy: What would happen if the toy factory ran out of energy?)

The children soon got into the game—knowing the answer (It will stop) and inventing similar questions.

Making a Big Book

Children drew pictures illustrating instances that appealed to them (see Figure 1). They assembled the pictures into a class big book called *What If The Cow Ran Out of Grass?*

Talking About Energy: What Does Energy Do?

The group tried defining energy not in terms of what it is, but what it does.
Chris explained that scientists use the word energy to describe all the different ways of making things go and making things hot. Scientists say that to make something hot or make something move or produce something, we need energy. We can identify where energy comes from (its source), as well as its effect.

Field Trip: What if the Baker's Electricity Went Off?

In the shopping center
On a field trip to a shopping center, the children continued the game, looking to see who uses energy and for what purpose: supermarkets, bakers, butchers, fast-food restaurants, houses, road repairers. The children compiled records of their findings: gas for cars, food for people, electricity for shops and factories.

Figure 1: A picture for a Big Book

Thinking about home

Back in class, children reviewed what they discussed on their field trip, and added to their lists data about home: energy for cooking, heat, hot water, laundry, etc. The key point Chris wanted the children to see was how much we depend on energy for survival and to maintain our way of life. At the same time, however, they compared sources: How many families cooked with gas? wood? electricity? How many different ways do homes use gas? electricity?

Science makes the difference

The children reflected on the idea that science was and is important in developing electricity and appliances, cars and trains, crops and farms, manufacturing. In some ways it helps make our lives better; in some ways it helps waste the Earth's resources.

Film and Books: Some People Are Running Out of Fuel

Chris used a short video, supported with pictures and books, to introduce the idea that shortages of food and fuel are major problems in some parts of the world and will become a problem for the world generally. For many people, shortages mean that life is "stopping."

Toward Solutions: What Can Be Done to Help?

The children suggested some possible solutions: better sharing, less waste, reduced use, new machines or fuels.

Chris prompted them to talk about how some of these solutions can be achieved—especially at a personal level (see Figure 2)—and some of the attempts at international aid.

Bringing It Together: Making a Little Book

Children told the stories they wanted to tell about energy, in each case starting with a What if? question. Their stories typically had three or four pages, with a picture and caption on each page.

Figure 2: Toward solutions

The Scientific Birthday Party

In this unit, children investigate different states of matter (liquid, solid, or gas), the properties of materials, and changes that occur during melting and freezing, evaporating and condensing.

The scene is set by a story about two silly chefs who confuse things like freezing and melting when they are preparing food for Freya's birthday party. The story provides the context for a range of food preparation activities in which students explore and identify properties of materials and how those properties can change.

The Story

TWO SILLY CHEFS TRY TO ORGANIZE A BIRTHDAY PARTY

It was Freya's birthday. She was going to be four years old. Her mom and dad hired two chefs to cater for the party. But the two chefs were quite silly.

First they tried to make popsicles. They put all of the ingredients into a bowl and mixed them carefully. They then poured the mixture into an ice cube tray and put popsicle sticks in the middle of each section. But they put the trays into the oven! What do you think happened?

Next they tried to make chocolate rabbits. They bought some chocolate blocks to melt

Materials

- Refrigerator.
- Materials for making popsicles of many kinds and flavors.
- Stove for cooking pizzas and cakes.
- Hot plate, pan, and glass saucepan for boiling water and melting chocolate and butter.
- Chocolate chips and molds for making chocolate shapes.
- Utensils—wooden spoons, ordinary spoons, measuring cups, cutting knives, and mixing bowls.
- Wheat and flour.
- Bowl and pestle (or blocks of wood).
- Pizza ingredients: bases (e.g., muffins), tomato paste (or sauce), grated cheese, chopped vegetables, pepperoni.
- Foods that dissolve (sugar, powdered sugar, salt, instant coffee), and others that don't (pepper, grated cheese, rice grains).
- Balloons.
- Paper to make chefs' hats.
- Cakes to serve at the birthday party.

Unit Outline

DAY	WHOLE GROUP ONE	INTRODUCED EXPERIENCES	WHOLE GROUP TWO
1	Read *Two Silly Chefs Try to Organize a Birthday Party.* Create a concept map of "Freezing."	Make popsicles from different substances. Watch some popsicles melt in the sun, in the warmth of the room, or on the stove.	Discuss freezing. Examine the frozen popsicles, and compare them to their liquid form.
2	Reread story. Create a concept map of "Melting."	Melt chocolate to pour into molds and make chocolate rabbits. Watch the chocolate turn to a solid again as it cools in the molds (and on the spoon).	Have children report on these activities. Compare molded chocolate and chocolate chips.
3	Reread story. Focus on the water boiling. Create a group concept map of "Steam."	Boil water in clear open dish. Make bread. Grind flour.	Have children report on these activities. Discuss making sand castles with flour and grinding wheat.
4	Reread story. Discuss how to make pizza.	Make pizza.	Have children report on this activity.
5	Reread story. Add the idea of putting sugar or salt in the tea. Create a group concept map of "Dissolving."	Try dissolving different substances in cold and warm water. Regain salt from solution by boiling away the water.	Ask groups to report orally on dissolving activities. Discuss what happens when sugar and salt dissolve.
6	Reread story. Create a group concept map of "Air."	Blow up balloons. Make chef hats for role play.	Role play the story of the *Two Silly Chefs.*
7	Role play the story.	Ice the birthday cake. Make minipizzas. Make bread. Blow up balloons.	Hold the birthday party.

• •

SUGGESTED AUSTRALIAN SCIENCE PROFILE OUTCOMES
The unit spans levels 1 and 2 in the strands:

• Natural and Processed Materials (Reactions and change; Structure and properties)
• Working scientifically (Conducting investigations; Processing data; Using science)

EXTENDING THE UNIT
The unit can readily be extended to include work at level 3 in each of these strands.

so that the liquid would fill the rabbit molds. However, they did not know very much about melting. They put the chocolate into the refrigerator instead of on top of the stove! What went wrong?

One important thing to make for the party was bread. First they collected some wheat. However, they did not know how to grind the wheat into flour. So they just put the solid grains of wheat into the bread mixture. What do you think happened?

The chefs thought the bread dough looked like it would make a good pizza crust, so they decided to make a pizza. For the topping, they chose cheese, onions, pineapple, and bacon. They put all of these solids, including the cheese, into the bottom of the pan. They then placed the dough over the top and poured the liquid tomato on top. What a mess! They were most confused. What should they have done?

The chefs thought they would make a nice pot of tea for all the moms and dads who were bringing their children to Freya's birthday party. First they found a big kettle. They knew there would be five people, so they measured five cups of water into the kettle. They then put the kettle on top of the stove and turned on the heat. They sat and watched the kettle boil and bubble. When they looked into the kettle they saw that it was empty. "What happened?" they asked.

Finally, they got around to decorating Freya's house for the birthday party. They bought a packet of balloons and set about putting them up. But they looked at each other and asked "What do you fill them with?" First they tried water. That did not work. Then they tried jellybeans. That did not work either. Finally they asked Freya's mom. She said they needed a gas to fill the balloons, not a liquid like water or a solid like jellybeans. "What sort of gas would you need?" they wanted to know. Can you help them?

When the children arrived at the party, they found a big mess instead of yummy food. However, it didn't matter, because Freya's birthday cake was so big that everyone could have three pieces.

Getting Started: Tell the Story

A child's world is full of substances that react and change. Those highlighted in the story are familiar to most young children. Yet the notion of materials changing from a solid to a liquid or a gas is complex.

Each child comes to school with different understanding and experiences. The story can be used as a stimulus to find out what children already know. Figure 1 charts the story elements, common misconceptions that children have, and the related scientific expressions of these properties.

Tell the *Two Silly Chefs Who Try to Organize a Birthday Party* story or a similar one. You might make the story into a book or series of posters. Try using the name of a child in your class instead of Freya.

The story sets up the unit, and links one day and activity to the others. Reread the story (or parts of it) each day, and ask a child or small group of children to report on the activities the students explore. With younger children, the reporting will be predominantly oral. Older children can use posters, books, or recipe cards to support their oral

STORY CONTENT	THE RESEARCH LITERATURE SUGGESTS THAT CHILDREN	PRESENTING SCIENTIFIC UNDERSTANDING
Making flour/grinding wheat—making bread. Making pizza—grating cheese; cutting up toppings; spreading tomato paste.	Are confused by powders. Some children think that because powders pour, they are not a solid.	Powders are usually considered to be a solid (though some scientists classify them as a separate state of matter, because a solid does not pour). A solid cannot be compressed. It has its own shape and rigidity.
Making popsicles from different substances (freezing and melting).	Think that liquids (many types) contain water.	Liquids are runny: they pour and usually take up the shape of their container. They cannot be compressed.
Decorating for the party—blowing up balloons.	Think air is a material.	Gases are mostly not visible. Gases spread out to fill the available space and do not have a shape. Gases can be compressed into a smaller space.
Making a cup of tea—boiling water.	Think that water vapor just disappears, goes into the receptacle which contains the water.	Boiling changes a liquid into a gas by heating. Bubbles of gas are formed all over the liquid, and the gas is released. A gaseous substance is called vapor.
Melting chocolate and making popsicles.	Have difficulty with change of states of matter: melting, freezing, evaporating, and condensing.	Melting changes a solid to a liquid by heating. Freezing changes a liquid to a solid by cooling. Evaporation changes a liquid to a vapor. Condensation changes a vapor to a liquid through cooling.

Table 1: **Relating the story to children's ideas**

presentations. All the children don't have to do each activity—they can learn about the others during the reporting sessions.

Activities

Make popsicles
Using ice trays, popsicle sticks, and a variety of liquids, (milk, cheese, chocolate, fruit juice, yogurt, pureed fruit) make nutritious and interesting popsicles.

Talk to the children about how the liquid's cooling causes it to turn into a solid. Have them touch the trays before and after they are put into the freezer so that they feel difference in temperature. Examine the different substances in the trays at different times during the freezing process so that students discover that some substances freeze faster than others and see firsthand the changes in structure and properties that occur as liquid freezes.

In their small groups, I gave the children the choice of putting their popsicles in the freezer or the oven. One child agreed during group time that "an oven heated and a freezer was for chilling," but other scientific concepts confused her. She insisted that for change to occur the popsicles must be put into an oven (as she had witnessed the change from liquid to solid in cake mixtures). It was only after she had seen the result of her yogurt popsicle in the hot oven that she was able to understand the concept of freezing.

Make chocolate rabbits

Using block chocolate and chocolate molds, make a selection of chocolates. Discuss with the children the concept of "melting." Talk to them about how the chocolate is being heated and this is causing it to change from a solid to a liquid. Do this with other foods such as butter.

Soo's students had a number of opposing views about melting and freezing, as the following transcript shows. Such differences set the context for trying out ideas that the silly chefs attempted.

Soo	(*reading the story*): Next they tried to make chocolate rabbits. They bought some chocolate blocks. However they did not know very much about melting. They put the chocolate into the refrigerator instead of on top of the stove! What went wrong?
Samantha:	They went hard.
Soo:	Why do you need to put the chocolate on to the stove?
Lauren:	So they can melt.
Ben:	Melt on the stove.
Altyn:	I said they won't. See, somebody put the chocolate bunny

	chocolates in the refrigerator and they melted.
Soo:	Do you think so?
Altyn:	Yes.
Cody:	They won't!
Lauren:	No.
Soo:	They would melt in the refrigerator?
Cody:	No they won't. They'll melt on the stove.
Soo:	What would happen if you put them on the stove?
Altyn:	Then, when you put them on the stove they get real hot, when you put them in the refrigerator they get, real, they get real soft and they, they get, ah, um. (*pause*)
Lauren:	Hard.
Jessica:	Hard.
Lazareth:	They get hard.
Soo:	Okay, we'll put your idea down, Altyn. They get
Altyn:	. . . real soft.
Soo:	They get soft in the refrigerator.
Altyn:	Yes, and they melt.
Teacher:	We might try this one day. They get soft in the refrigerator.
Altyn:	And they melt.
Cody:	No they don't!!!
Altyn:	Yes they do!!
Lauren:	No they don't!
Soo:	Listen, that's all right Cody. We're going to try this, we're going to make some chocolate bunnies sometime so we'll try it and see what happens. Okay? We'll work it out.

Blow up balloons

Try out the activities listed in the story. Fill the balloons with water, jellybeans, and other substances. Talk about how air is a gas and is a material even though it cannot be seen.

Boil water

Water is a particularly good material for helping children understand about solids, liquids and gases, since it is easy to change the state of water. Talk to the children about how the water changes from a liquid into a gas when it boils. The water vapor above the liquid forms "clouds" as it cools in the air; water vapor in the boiling liquid can be seen as bubbles of gas.

Soo found that children were fascinated by water boiling in a clear glass dish (Figure 1). They could watch it for thirty minutes at a time, seeing the bubbles form and rise (some of the children called it soda). They watched clouds form in the steam above the dish and passed their hands through the clouds, collecting water droplets as the water vapor condensed on their skin.

It was important to provide equipment that helped the children see and understand what was taking place. The glass dish did that. The children needed to know that what was happening was not a 'magic trick' or an unexplainable event. Some children inspected the hot plate afterward to see if any water had leaked out that way. We put a shallow pool of water in the dish and watched it 'disappear.' Another useful piece of equipment was a cold pane of glass, which we held over the steam. The children could see condensation taking place, water droplets forming on the glass. They squealed with delight.

Discuss changes that aren't melting and freezing

Sometimes liquids change to solids in other ways than by freezing. For example, a cake mixture and bread dough turn solid in the oven; plaster and concrete mixtures turn solid as they "set."

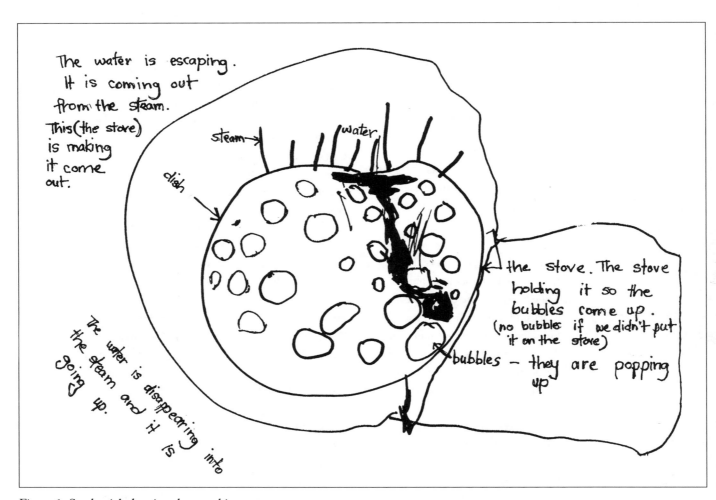

Figure 1: Stephanie's drawing about making steam

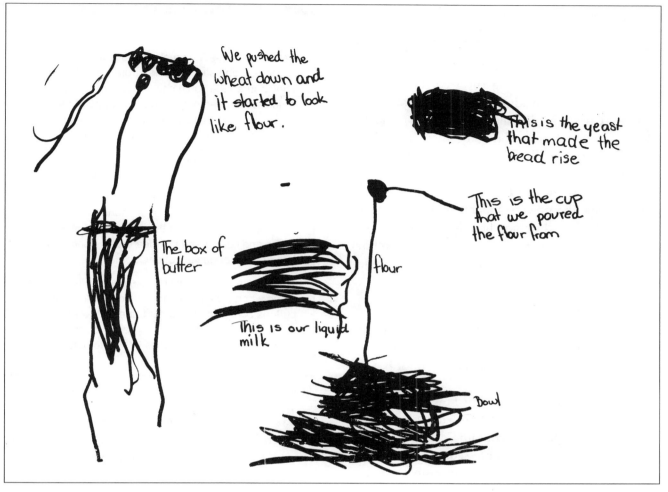

We pushed the wheat down and it started to look like flour.

This is the yeast that made the bread rise

This is the cup that we poured the flour from

The box of butter

flour

This is our liquid milk

Bowl

Figure 2: **Jessica makes bread**

One distinction between these processes and melting/freezing is that they are not reversible. Heating the cake mix turns it to solid, but cooling it does not make it liquid again. Chemical reactions have taken place. Soo decided not to make issues of these distinctions but to keep them in mind as possible sources of confusion.

Children can also be confused about the difference between melting and dissolving: sugar "disappears" when it is mixed into water. Soo's students stirred into water some solids that dissolve, such as sugar and salt, and some that don't, such as pepper and grated cheese. They compared dissolving things in cold water and hot water. To see that dissolving is reversible, they put some salty water in a Pyrex dish and evaporated away the water. They could taste the salt that was left.

Make bread and make pizzas

Help children understand that when a solid is ground (or grated) it is still called a solid. Children become confused because the ground or grated substance can pour, so they think of it as a liquid. The key idea is that melting something is different from cutting it into tiny pieces.

Make bread or pizza dough by using wheat that the children have ground up (Figure 2). Try out recipes that use grated things such as cheese and carrots. Chop up several kinds of things for pizza toppings. This will help children understand the concepts of solids and liquids.

Make a birthday cake

If a student has a birthday during the unit, celebrate it with a birthday tea or lunch. On the day of the party, read the story using the child's name. Icing the cake (and making the icing), making bread, making minipizzas (bases of English muffins work well), and decorating the room bring together all the things the children have been doing in a fun way!

Play *What Am I?*

Describe objects and have children decide whether they are liquids, solids, or gases. Use the following information in combination with the characteristics of the object you are describing:

- Solids: I can be a hard block or I can be soft and sometimes I can even be powdery. I take up a space and I have my own shape. I cannot be compressed.
- Liquids: I am runny. I take up a definite amount of space. I usually take up the shape of the container I am in. I cannot be compressed.
- Gases: I am mostly not visible. I can spread out in all directions to fill all the available space. I have no shape. I can be compressed into smaller spaces.

Bringing Ideas Together: Concept Mapping

Concept maps can be used at various points in the unit to help the children relate ideas.

There are many different ways of making concept maps: children can build out from a central word like "freezing"; brainstorm ideas and then group them; take instances or examples and put them under headings; sort pictures into hoops on the floor, then link the ideas with streamers or yarn.

Anthony, trying the unit with his first graders, asked them to write words to do with freezing on cards. He had prepared long

On Tuesday, as part of science, the children made Easter Bunnies. They melted chocolate in a saucepan, and saw it change from a solid to liquid. They poured the liquid chocolate into the moulds, and watched it spread out, taking the shape of the mould. They saw that, as it cooled, it turned back to a solid, and could now hold the shape of the mould.

Instead of little buttons of solid chocolate, now we had Easter bunnies! We can use science to help us do things we want to do!

As well as noticing how things change when they are heated, we talked about the differences between solids and liquids and the idea that melting and freezing are opposites of each other.

Then came time for tasting. Did chocolate taste the same when it was solid and liquid? When it was in buttons compared to Easter bunnies? Nearly everyone felt it tasted best as Easter bunnies. Could we make the Easter bunnies back into buttons? Nobody wanted to!

Figure 3: Newsletter extract

arrows cut from a colored card. After the children had all read their words aloud, he asked one child to place her card on the carpet. Those who thought their word would fit with that one took an arrow and put it and their card on the carpet, explaining the connection. Other children followed until all of the cards had been used and each child had had a turn. This technique generated a lot of discussion among the children, a lot of learning for children and teacher, and a class web the students could refer back to and revise during the unit.

Linking Home and School

Soo kept in contact with the children's families through a weekly newsletter (an extract is shown in Figure 3) and by talking with parents each morning when they brought their children to school. One parent wanted help explaining the difference between solids and liquids, since liquids pour but so do powders. Together, Soo and the parent decided that a solid can hold its own shape (as can powders to some extent), whereas liquids take the shape of the container they are in.

Soo's Reflections

This unit was challenging yet rewarding with my group of preschool children, and I'm confident it would work well with older children, with whom you could go further with things like the distinction between melting and dissolving and when changes are reversible.

The unit was challenging in the sense that my own scientific understanding had to be refined so that my teaching was clear and focused. I had to understand where the children were so that my teaching was tuned to their level of understanding.

The reward came when the children exclaimed excitedly to their mom or dad what they had found out.

Extensions and Variations

Many extensions of the unit are possible. You could address other science ideas such as heat or build in other curriculum areas such as health, technology, or creative writing. Children could write a similar story around a different feast, like Thanksgiving, or add other episodes to this story. For example, Kerry and Sonya suggested that the chefs could make jelly and leave it outside to cool but the dog gets to it.

As a technological extension, students could tackle the question How can we make the popsicle sticks sit in the middle of the popsicle mixture?

The Teddy Bears' Barbecue

A barbecue is a favorite childhood experience that can enable a great deal of scientific learning about observable changes children are familiar with but do not necessarily understand:

- Burning (wood and food).
- Decaying (food, leaf litter).
- Dissolving (washing up, with and without soap).
- Melting and solidifying (fat from the meat).
- Sunburn.

A picnic also provides opportunities for children to use their senses—watching, smelling, touching, hearing, and tasting—and to think about responsible action for protecting the environment and caring for living things.

Getting Started

What's it all about?

Peta began with *The Three Bears*, using toy bears and doll furniture. She made a few changes to the story line:

THE THREE BEARS, BUT WITH A DIFFERENCE!

PETA:	In the dark, dark woods there lived three bears (*shows toy bears*). There was a great big bear with a great big voice! There was a middle-sized bear with a middle-sized voice, and a teeny tiny bear with a teeny tiny voice. One day the middle-sized bear decided to make some porridge for breakfast. What do you think the middle-sized bear had to use to make porridge?
ALBERT:	Some water.
PETA:	Some water. There is some water.
THERESA:	Some milk to cool it off.
PETA:	Some milk to cool it off. Yes, good idea. (*Puts water into pot and holds up porridge packet*) A little bit of water and some . . . who knows what this is?

Materials

- Food and equipment for a barbecue picnic—barbecue utensils, clear plastic cups, food containers, plastic plates, wash-up solvents (soap, liquid detergent, powdered detergent), bucket, sausages, bread, butter, salad, fruit.
- Ingredients for making teddy bear biscuits (flour, sugar, butter) and a stove for cooking.

Unit Outline

DAYS	WHOLE GROUP ONE	INTRODUCED EXPERIENCES	WHOLE GROUP TWO
1–6	Tell the story *The Three Bears*. Suggest an invitation to the teddy bears' barbecue. Create concept maps of "barbecue" and "changes we will see."	Ask children to write their own invitation to the teddy bears' barbecue. Classify the drinks the children will bring to the barbecue. Make teddy bear biscuits. Collect fruit scraps and make a series of compost bins.	Retell the story; role-play *The Three Bears*.
7	Hold the teddy bears' barbecue field trip.	Lay the fire and burn wood. Go on a rust hunt. Cook the sausages. Take a nature walk. Clean up.	Singing game: Going on a bear hunt. Read *Bears in the Night*, by Stan and Jan Berenstain (New York: Random House Books for Young Readers, 1971)
8	Reread *Bears in the Night*. Play the singing game *We're Going on a Bear Hunt*. Talk about what happened at the teddy bears' barbecue.	Set a fire in the outdoor area—burn wood; toast and burn bread; burn paper straws. Moisten steel wool and leave on tray for daily observations. Place fruit scraps on tray and leave for daily observations. Moisten bread and leave on tray for daily observations.	Write group story of *The Teddy Bear Barbecue*, using photos, chart paper, and an easel.
9	Reread group story (with pictures and text mounted into book).	Look through fire site for charcoal and ash. Draw pictures on pavement with charcoal. Observe steel wool, fruit scraps, and bread.	Talk about the fire site.
10–18		Organize a compost bin for all food scraps (later start a vegetable garden, using compost).	Discuss observations.

SUGGESTED AUSTRALIAN SCIENCE PROFILE
OUTCOMES
The unit spans levels 1 and 2 in the strands:

• Natural and Processed Materials (Reactions
and change; Structure and properties)
• Working Scientifically (Conducting
investigations; Processing data; Acting
responsibly)

DYLAN: Porridge.
Story continues: making porridge, the bears finding it too hot . . .
Enter Goldilocks, who tries porridge, chairs and beds, and is discovered, asleep.
PETA: The teeny tiny bear said, "Don't be frightened. Would you stay with us?" The middle-sized bear added, "We were planning to go on a barbecue, would you like to come with us?" "Could I?" asked Goldilocks. "We were just writing the invitations," said the middle-sized bear. "I will go over and get it and read it to you." (*She shows the invitation* [see Figure 1] *to the toy bears and the children, then reads it aloud.*)

What do children already know about changes they will see?

To find out what the children already know as you plan the details, ask them what they think will happen at the teddy bear barbecue.

PETA: What do you think will happen at the teddy bear barbecue?
LESLIE: I think we are going to have a lot of fun!
PETA: What do you think you do on a barbecue?
CHRISTINE: You make a fire.
PETA: How do you think you would make a fire?
LESLIE: Bring some tissues with you. (*Discussion about lighting a fire*)

PETA: What shall we cook at the barbecue?
CASSANDRA: Sausages!
PETA: What things could we take along to the barbecue?
RAY: Some matches.
CASSANDRA: Sausages.
LESLIE: Drinks.
PETA: Shall we take some milk along?
LESLIE: Yes.
PETA: If it is a warm day, what could happen to the milk? (*No response*)
PETA: Perhaps we may need to do some investigating into which drinks will be okay to take on a picnic. What other things could we take along to the barbecue?
CASSANDRA: Hats.
RAY: Sun screen.
PETA: Hats. Yes, a good idea. And sun screen. What happens to our skin when it is not protected? (*Discussion about sunburn*)
PETA: Do you think we should take some things to clean up, such as detergent?
RAY: Yes, and I can do the dishes! (*Discussion about what is used for doing dishes and what happens; children are encouraged Go observe parents doing the dishes that night*)

I felt at this stage many of the children were losing concentration because they were very excited. I wanted to find out what the children thought about rusting, burning, and decaying, but I decided to leave this to tomorrow when they were less excitable. Next day, the children and I made a concept map [see Figure 2] of changes that we might see at the barbecue. The discussion helped to cue them in for the barbecue and being scientists. It also helped me with planning, as I had a better idea about what the children understood.

Dear

We are going on a Teddy Bear's Barbeque.

We would love you to come!

Remember to bring your teddy and to wear playclothes and a sunhat.

We're going to do lots of exciting things (like building a fire).

Please let us know if you can come.

Love from

Bear xxx

P.S. Remember to put all rubbish in the bin!

Figure 1: Invitation

Planning the Barbecue

The barbecue field trip was the stimulus for the entire unit and set the context for learning in a variety of ways about materials and change. Before the barbecue, Peta inspected the barbecue site, worked through details of the unit plan, organized and completed work that needed to be done before the excursion, and planned both the site and the follow-up activities. She wanted to incorporate a range of across-the-curriculum experiences:

- Writing the invitation.
- Retelling the story using the children's teddy bears.
- Role-playing *The Three Bears*.
- Collecting fruit scraps each day and constructing a series of compost bins (labeled "Day 1," "Day 2," etc.).
- Taking a survey of the children's favorite drinks (juice, milk, water).
- Placing the liquids into clear plastic cups, putting them on the window sill, and marking on a calendar the days the drinks are left out of the refrigerator.
- Washing up with different solvents (bar soap, liquid detergent, powdered detergent) and without (in just water). (She had the children wash their fruit bowls and lunch boxes, cooking containers [including some that had held oil-based ingredients], and the home corner crockery.)
- Washing and hanging out doll clothes.
- Designing and making bear homes.
- Bathing the home corner dolls.
- Making teddy bear biscuits.

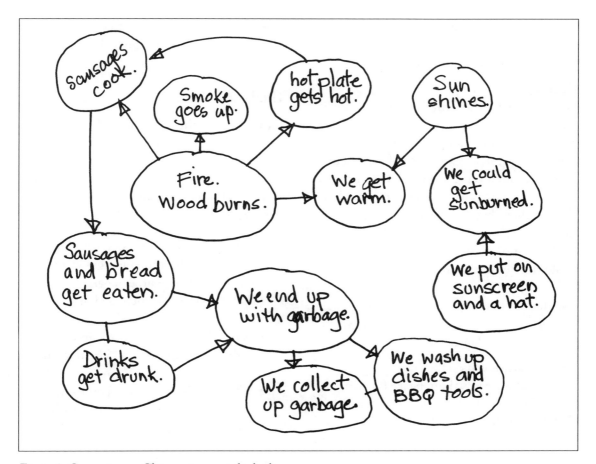

Figure 2: Concept map: Changes to see at the barbecue

Activities at the Site

Lay the fire

The site had firewood and fireplaces. The children collected firewood as a group. Peta discussed with them how to be environmentally responsible with regard to wood and fire. They looked for evidence of previous fires, realizing that charcoal and ash are parts of a fire (in addition to wood, smoke, flames, and heat).

Once the fire was laid, the children listed the changes they expected would happen once they lit it. Then they watched, listened, smelt and felt: What can you see happening to the wood? Is it still the same size? Is it still the same color? Would it feel different if you touched it? What smells have you noticed? and What can you feel?

The chemical changes that occur dur-ing burning are difficult to explain to young children. Peta focused on the physical changes and on what happened to the wood, encouraging the children to think more broadly than the wood's just disappearing.

When I organized the barbecue I had to make sure there was enough ash and charcoal from previous fires for the children to explore. This was not as easy as I had first thought. I brought along a large bag of ash and planted it around the picnic site and asked the children if they could find any evidence of burnt wood from previous fires.

Go on a rust hunt

Picnic sites usually include interesting litter. Some of the children went on a rust hunt. This helped them see that only certain metals rust—for example, steel does, but aluminum does not. Rusting is a complex concept. It is enough for young children to identify rust and to associate it with iron and steel.

Cooking

Peta talked to the children about how in most cases the cooking process cannot easily be reversed. For example, before the excursion, the children made teddy bear biscuits. Once the flour, egg, sugar, and water were combined and cooked, it was impossible to change them back. Similarly, on the excursion, the children watched the sausages cooking and discussed how the burnt ones could not be "unburnt."

> We had a lot of fun inventing ways to try and change things back again. None of which were successful, I might add!

Take a nature walk

The children took their bears for a nature walk. They looked particularly for things that were rotting and decaying—twigs and fallen branches, leaf litter, animal droppings, perhaps even dead animals. Peta asked the children to explain how they knew the material was decaying.

Clean up

The explorations the children had done into detergents before the excursion helped them decide how to wash up all the fatty crockery. The washing-up activity was in great demand!

While the children were cleaning up, Peta talked about how food rots. The picnic site had decomposing food in the garbage cans (you can bring a few examples along if you think there won't be anything there). This was not only a good visual experience for the children but also an excellent olfactory one! The children talked about what they thought was happening—whether decay was due to the air, temperature, microbes, or all of these things. Peta related the discussion to decay they had seen in garden compost and

talked about the importance of decay in "removing" wastes and providing nutrients for plants.

Back at School

At the end of the day when all of the teddy bears and their owners returned to school, Peta asked the children to report from their teddy bears' perspective—what the teddy bears understood about changes they had observed:

- What changes to the sausages did Teddy see when the sausages were cooking on the barbecue grill?
- What changes to the wood did Teddy notice?
- What things did Teddy see in the garbage cans? How could he tell what they were?
- What did Teddy see happen to the oily containers when you tried to wash them up with just water?

On the following day, I showed the children some of the burnt food, a few rusty horseshoes and bottle tops, and a small bucket with rotting fruit scraps. This prompted instant recall. Most children seemed to understand burning and associated this with the black. One child explained how the wood changed in the flames to charcoal and ashes. The greatest learning and understanding seemed to come from the rusty horseshoes. Children really seemed to pick up on the word rusty and could label something as rusty. On the other hand, when I showed them the bucket of rotting scraps they described what they saw and smelt as "green, yucky, smelly, old and dirty." Their understanding here seemed to be still limited.

Peta's follow-up activities included observing fruit scraps rotting, steel wool rusting, bread molding, and wood burning. The highlight for the children was creating a whole-group book about their experience, which they re-read on many occasions.

Peta's Reflections

The children enjoyed the unit immensely. It was an excellent vehicle for integrating ideas from across the curriculum and encouraging the children to use the whole range of their senses, think about how they respond to different experiences, and notice changes that go on in their environment. With its focus on observing changes, the science outcomes of the unit relate more to raising awareness of some scientific ideas than full understanding—the changes are too complex. The point is more to encourage them to notice changes at this stage and lay a foundation for future work in explaining them.

Egbert, What Do You Know About Rain?

Because children have so many experiences with water in their everyday life, learning experiences related to water are very attractive. Children can explore:

- The water cycle (evaporation and condensation)
- Why objects float and sink in water.
- The concept of dissolving.

This unit and the next two focus on these three aspects of water. This first unit concentrates on the water cycle:

- Physical phenomena such as rain, sun, clouds, rivers, and lakes.
- Heating, evaporation, and condensation.
- Distinguishing between changes that cannot be readily reversed and those that can.
- The idea that water is continually recycled.

Katrina's version of the unit is presented in detail. It is summarized in the table on page 63. For her group Egbert was a puppet. Janet's approach is summarized in the table on pages 69–70. For her, Egbert was an alien.

Getting Started: What Do We Already Know About Water?

Setting the scene

Egbert wants to know about water, but he doesn't know very much yet. Katrina introduces Egbert as follows:

Materials

- Egbert, a puppet (optional).
- Cartons, tubs, and blocks.
- Stones, feathers, plants, etc. (things found near a river).
- Spoons and plates.
- Hot plate and glass saucepan.
- Large funnel; plastic tubing; ice in a plastic bag; jar to collect water; stands, blocks and pegs to secure the equipment in place.
- Felt board, chart paper, and easel.
- Rain gauge, flag or wind sock (a sock on a coat hanger is a no-frills substitute), thermometer.
- Pictures of different cloud types.
- Sandbox, bucket of water, plastic sheeting, diagram of the water cycle (clouds, raindrops, sun, dam, river).
- Sheet, broom handle (for mast), steering wheel.

Unit Outline

The unit draws strongly on the children's experience and ideas by introducing a puppet, Egbert, (If you prefer, you can pretend to be an alien from another planet) who knows nothing about water. The children try to explain to Egbert about water; Egbert keeps asking "silly" questions. The discussions are supplemented by activities, texts, concept maps, and role plays to show relationships.

The unit has five sections:

- Getting started: What do we already know about water?
- Presenting the water cycle
- Investigating aspects of the water cycle
- Linking home and school
- Putting it together: What have we learned?

SUGGESTED AUSTRALIAN SCIENCE PROFILE OUTCOMES
The unit spans levels 1 and 2 in the strands:

- Earth, Sky, and Beyond (Earth, sky, and people; The changing Earth)
- Natural and Processed Materials (Structure and properties; Reactions and change)
- Working Scientifically (Processing data; Using science)

LINKS TO OTHER UNITS:
- A Watery Treasure Hunt (floating and sinking).
- Oh, No Quickie the Cat Dissolved! (dissolving).
- The Scientific Birthday Party (liquids, solids and gases).
- Making Dirt (the formation and effects of rivers).
- They Don't Tell the Truth About the Wind (investigating weather).

KATRINA: This is my friend, Egbert. Do you think you could say good morning to Egbert?

CHILDREN: Good morning, Egbert.

EGBERT: Good morning, everyone.

CHILDREN: (*Laughter*) That's funny.

KATRINA: Do you know why Egbert has come here today? What are you doing here this morning Egbert?

EGBERT: I've heard that there are very, very clever children in this group.

CHILDREN: (*Laughter*)

KATRINA: Who told you that?

EGBERT: I just heard.

KATRINA: Is he right?

CHILDREN: Yes! (*Laughter*)

EGBERT: Well, you know I am a bit embarrassed because I don't know very much. And I would really like to learn lots of things from you. Do you think you could help me learn?

CHILDREN: Yes!

EGBERT: That makes me feel much better. To start with, there is something over here (*motions to a container of water*) . . .

CHILDREN: Water! Liquid!

EGBERT: Liquid? What's liquid?

CHILDREN: Water!

KATRINA: Water. Don't you know what water is, Egbert?

EGBERT: (Shakes head to indicate no.)

KATRINA: Do you think we could write it up so Egbert could remember?

CHILDREN: Yes!

Finding out what children already know

As the children explain to Egbert about water and rain, Katrina assembles a concept map of their ideas, using chart paper on an easel (see Figure 1).

KATRINA: Egbert, you sit up here (*puts puppet on easel*) and watch, while we write up all the things we know about water. Then you can take the paper home.
(*To children*) What were some of

DAY	WHOLE GROUP ONE	INTRODUCED EXPERIENCES	WHOLE GROUP TWO
1	Explain "water" to Egbert. Prepare a group concept map. Prepare a diagram of the water cycle.	Make a boat in which to float down a pretend river. Discuss children's previous experiences. Boil water and collect water vapor on the back of a spoon. Have each child draw a concept map of his or her understanding of the water cycle.	Climb into boat and float down a pretend river. Discuss children's previous experiences.
2	Have children tell Egbert about their activities on the previous day—steam and spoons; making a block boat. Discuss the type of protective clothing needed for the boat trip.	Set up a sandbox lake. Prepare take-home books and plan observations of water evaporation and drying.	Draw picture on easel of weather conditions. Read a story about the water cycle. Retell the story of the water cycle using the diagram prepared earlier.
3	*Role play:* Weather report (oral and written); boat trip.	Observe water evaporation in the sandbox lake. Make rain: set up the distillation apparatus and ask children to predict what will happen.	Oral report: How did we make rain?

Table 1: Katrina's approach

the things you told me about water?
CHILDREN: It's a liquid.
KATRINA: Do you think Egbert will know what a liquid is? What do you think a liquid is?
CHILDREN: A drink. It stays in a puddle.
EGBERT: You told me that this stuff here (*points to the container of water*) is water, and it's a liquid, so it can stay in a puddle, but where does it come from?
CHILDREN: A tap. From a big river.
STEPHANIE: Up there, there was a place that

was so big, it was enormous, and even bigger than a house, even bigger than Monica's house. It has a drain thing; when you turned the tap on, it comes from the big place.
EGBERT: You told me that the water comes from the tap. How does it get into the tap?
JOSHUA: From the pipes.
EGBERT: How does it get into the pipes?
JOSHUA: From a river.
EGBERT: How does it get into the river?
JESSICA: From the rain.

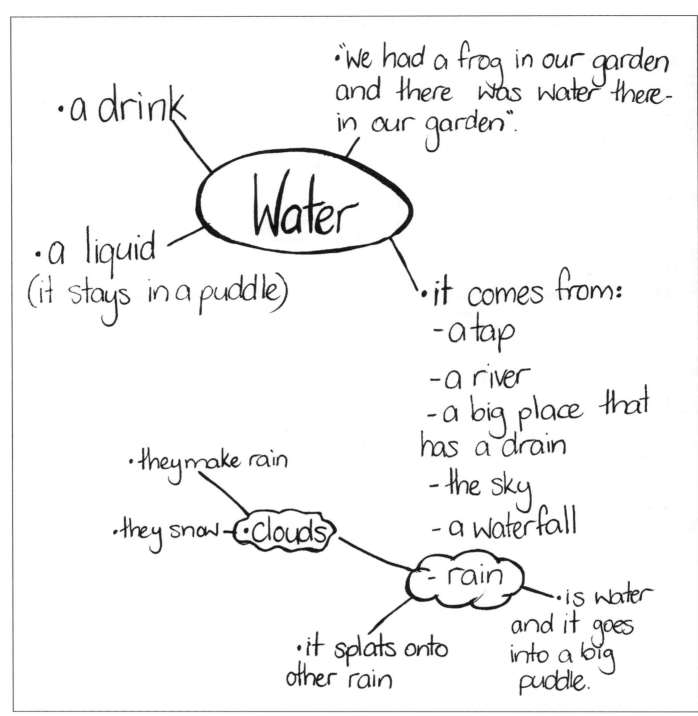

Figure 1: Concept map

STEPHANIE: From a big waterfall.

EGBERT: What is rain?

JESSICA: Rain is water. And it goes into a big puddle.

JOSHUA: Yeah, because it splats on to another rain. (*Holds hands close together*)

EGBERT: Where does rain come from?

CHILDREN: From clouds. Clouds, they make rain.

EGBERT: But what are clouds?

CHILDREN: Clouds are what know. Clouds make the rain.

Some of the children have well-developed views regarding water. For example, Stephanie is on the brink of the idea of the water cycle. The group had investigated boiling water and steam in the earlier unit, *The Scientific Birthday Party.*

EGBERT: How does the cloud make the rain?
STEPHANIE: Steam.
EGBERT: Steam?
STEPHANIE: Steam carries rain up into the sky and then things, like the clouds, and then it rains.
EGBERT: And what makes the steam go up?

Presenting the Water Cycle

Katrina uses pictures on a bulletin board to explain the water cycle. This presentation indicates to the children where the unit is headed, summarizes many of the ideas they have expressed, and provides an additional stimulus to explore their understandings. The children manipulate the pictures of clouds, water droplets, rivers, and the sun as they discuss the water cycle (see Figure 2).

Investigating Aspects of the Water Cycle

Going sailing
Katrina uses the role play of sailing down a river to tie together different parts of the unit.

The children, using wooden blocks, construct an imaginary boat, big enough for everyone to fit in. Load everyone on board. Row or sail down your imaginary river.

Figure 2: Ruben's drawing of the water cycle

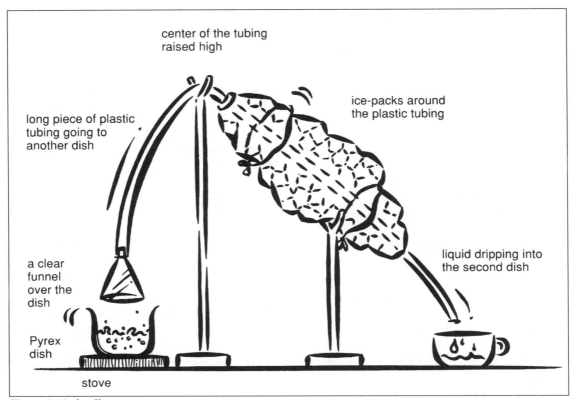

Figure 3: A distillation apparatus

Stop at points along the way. The children go ashore and pretend to find things they brought for show-and-tell, imaginary things, things Katrina introduces: gravel and stones, a feather, a piece of drift wood, a soda can. How did they get into the river? For that matter, how did the water get into the river? Have you ever been near a river that runs fast? runs slow?

The role play highlights the ideas that rain runs into rivers and that rivers flow downhill to other rivers, lakes, and the sea. It is also a window into children's experiences and knowledge—the children are likely to report on things they have found near water in the past.

Role-playing a weather report
In preparation for a second trip, think about the weather. Focus on things getting wet in the rain and things drying out in the sun and wind.

Katrina's group role-plays a weather report and discusses how they can prepare for a safe journey—protection from rain, sun and drowning. Later the children go outside and observe the weather as a way of preparing for the trip. They look at and/or feel the wind, rain, and sunlight; they notice clouds and try to predict whether it will rain. (The unit "They Don't Tell the Truth About the Wind" develops further understanding of weather.)

Making a sandbox lake
Investigate how water evaporates from the water surface. In the spirit of the river cruise, link ideas to the river (as well as oceans, lakes, plants, etc.). Make a pond or lake in the sandbox. Use a shallow bowl to put the water in and push the sand around it (otherwise seepage may confuse the children) and mark the water level over time. Similarly, look at a puddle of rain and mark the changes.

The sandbox is also a good prompt for talking about the way rivers form as rain runs down from the mountains and how rivers can cause erosion. The children can build mountain ranges and pour water (or sprinkle it from a watering can) on to the top of them. They can also make dams and reservoirs (using plastic bags to stop seepage). Activities in the sandbox and ideas of erosion are part of the unit *Making Dirt*.

Making a model of the water cycle

The notion of water evaporating, becoming invisible, then rising up to become visible again as clouds and rain is a fascinating one for children. It is also difficult. To make it more concrete, Katrina sets up the model shown in Figure 3.

Janet, on the other hand, sets up a clear, sealed plastic bag near the window (see Figure 4). The small amount of water in the bottom of the bag soon evaporates. An ice pack near the top causes condensation, which then runs down inside the bag, back to the pond at the bottom. The children observe as well the additional condensation that occurs overnight, and liken it to dew that forms on the lawns and cars and bikes outside.

Linking Home and School

The children take home booklets with ideas to try with their parents and things to observe. The activities are linked directly to ones they are doing at school.

The activity booklets give parents an opportunity to become involved with their children's schoolwork and to discuss in a more direct way the things their child has been doing in school.

Christine's mom sends in this message with her book: "Christine was (and still is) very proud about sharing what she learned during science this week. Not only will she share with family, but with friends and virtual strangers (to her) as well."

Katrina also reports in the school bulletin some of the things children are doing and suggestions that parents can try.

Putting It Together: What Have We Learned?

Back to the bulletin board

Katrina reads to the children from a book on how clouds are formed.

With the help of the earlier water-cycle diagram, the children retell the story, linking it to ideas of their own and the activities they have done (Figure 5). Katrina focuses on the idea that cooling causes water vapor to condense from the air and to form water droplets. When these tiny droplets of water in the clouds collide with one another, they join, forming bigger drops which fall as rain.

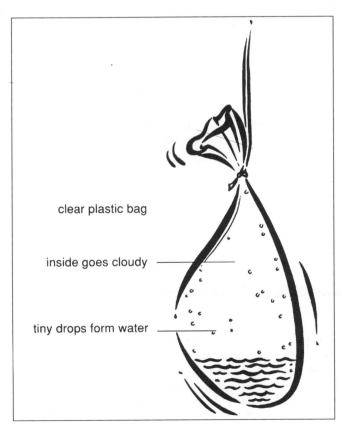

clear plastic bag

inside goes cloudy

tiny drops form water

Figure 4

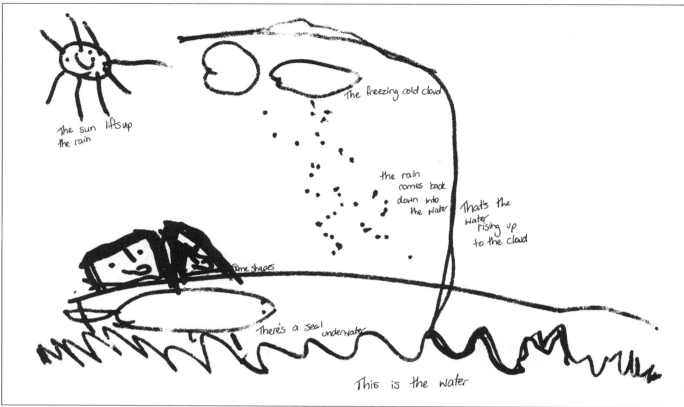

The sun lifts up the rain

The freezing cold cloud

the rain comes back down into the water

That's the water rising up to the cloud

Some shapes

There's a seal underwater

This is the water

Figure 5: Stephanie's water cycle

Katrina's Reflections

The children responded really well to the whole teaching sequence (especially Egbert). It was great to see the development in their thinking from what they had originally shared for the group concept map 'when clouds clap their hands - that is thunder and that is what makes rain!' through to the end of the sequence where they could talk clearly about the water cycle. It reminded me that children should never be underestimated. I think also it can be valuable to introduce complex ideas in a meaningful context before confusion sets in.

DAY 1

To begin the unit I took a container of water and put it in front of the children and pretended that I was a visitor from outer space who had never seen water before and asked them what it was. We made a concept map with all their responses. I found that by continually asking "but why?" "What else do you know?", or "how?" the children extended their ideas and thinking and delighted in teaching me! We finished the session at the point where the children felt "Water comes from rain."

Table 2: Janet's approach

DAY 2

In the first session the children concluded that water comes from rain. As a result, I asked the children to tell me about rain. A number of unusual ideas emerged:

• Rain comes from dark clouds.
• The rain goes into the water fountain hole in the night time so there is water to drink when we are at school.
• Rain goes in the creek and the motor sucks the water out.
• Gravity makes the rain come down.
• The rain goes through the earth up into the mountains and into the clouds.
• The clouds come down really low and suck the water up and then it goes into the sky.
• The clouds drink the water, then squeeze it out again.
• The clouds suck up the water because it hasn't any gravity in it.

At this point I showed a poster of the water cycle and likened it to their previous work on paper recycling in our school. This prompted some of the children to call the process water recycling. We then looked in a number of books on rain and the water cycle.

DAY 3

On the third day we tried a role play. The children and I set the room up with a mat as the water, and a row of small chairs, large chairs, and then the desks to enable the water vapor to rise. The children knew that we needed the sun to warm the water. We talked about other things we needed, like tiny raindrops. We selected children to be the sun, the river, and dam water. As the sun shone, the water vapor (children) rose up on to the first layer of chairs, getting colder. As more water evaporated, the water at the low level (children on small chairs) rose to a higher level (children moved to the bigger chairs). The sun continued to shine, the water vapor continued to rise, and eventually all of the "water children" were in dark clouds (on the desks). They were very crowded and became very heavy. Then they all fell to the ground, where they had started. We repeated this drama session many times, followed by story writing and artwork.

DAYS 4–7

Through looking at and reading the range of books in our class, the children could see many everyday examples of water evaporation and condensation. We discussed

• Boiling a kettle.
• Boiling water in a pot until the pot was empty.
• Mirrors fogging in the bathroom.

Over the week we

• Collected water vapor on the back of a spoon.
• Put two saucers with a teaspoon of water in each in the sun, but covered one saucer and watched to see what would happen.
• Made a rain cycle in a plastic bag (see Figure 5) and put it in the sun.
• Used distillation apparatus (see Figure 4) to make a water cycle system.

DAY 8

To end the unit, each child drew a picture to give to the visitor from outer space, explaining where rain came from and how water was recycled. The activity enabled the children to summarize what they had learned and me to see the progress they had made.

Table 2: continued

A Watery Treasure Hunt

This unit is the second in a series of three on water. Floating and sinking are phenomena that almost all children have experienced and enjoy. This unit helps them reflect on that experience. However, an understanding of floating and sinking will take children many years to develop, because the concepts are complex. In this unit, children:

- Have experiences with water.
- Sort out floaters and sinkers.
- Recognize that a floater can be made to sink (a boat with a hole in it, a boat with too big a load) and a sinker can be made to float (attaching it to a floater, reshaping it).
- See that when things float they are not "on top of the water" but part in, part out.
- Feel the force of water pushing up on a floating object (e.g., a ball)—floating is caused by the water itself.

This unit is not designed to teach the underlying principles of floating and sinking—that will come later.

The unit is built around a problem-solving situation: a farmer loads animals onto a boat to save them from an imminent storm, but she puts too many animals on the boat

and it sinks. The question for the children is "Who sank the boat?" This leads to investigations into floating and sinking—determining which objects sink and which float, attaching objects to sinkers that make them float and vice versa, and so on.

Getting Started: The Farmer Crosses the Lake

Set Up the Problem
Construct a long lake in the sandbox, or simulate it with a baby's bathtub or rectangular

Materials

- Sandbox and plastic sheet and/or tubs.
- Plastic and wooden farm animals and people.
- Materials (wood, plastic, clay, paper, cardboard) for making boats.
- Objects that float (wooden blocks, pieces of styrofoam, balls, balloons, apples) and ones that sink (marbles, clay, stones, kitchen utensils).
- Large ice-cream containers or buckets.
- Cloths and sponges.

Unit Outline

DAY	WHOLE GROUP ONE	INTRODUCED EXPERIENCES	WHOLE GROUP TWO
1	Tell a story in the sandbox: "The Day of the Storm."	Make boats to put into the sandpit lake. Have each child draw a concept map of her or his understanding of floating and sinking.	
2	Retell "The Day of the Storm." Discuss which items could float across to the other side of the lake and which things would sink and would need a boat to take them over.	Make boats to put into the sandpit lake. Sort objects into those that float, those that sink, and those that children are unsure about.	Discuss items that float and sink. Generate questions for investigation.
3	Answer some of the children's questions about who sank the boat.	Investigations: • Make different types of boats. • Make a submarine. • Test ideas about who sank the boat.	Use puppets to tell the story "Who Sank the Boat?" Report back to the whole group (include demonstrations).

dishes of water placed end to end. Have the children sit in a circle around the "lake."

Using three different types of boats, plastic farm animals, and a plastic family as props, tell the story of a farmer and her family crossing the lake to safety because of an imminent storm (songs like "I Hear Thunder," "Rain, Rain, Go Away," and "Have You Seen the Wind Today?" will add to the story). Use the boats to load the farm animals and the people. (This could also lead to discussions about water safety—particularly the ideas of lifejackets and life buoys.)

Raise the question of floaters and sinkers

At the end of the story, ask the children to predict which story props could have floated across anyway and would not have needed a boat. The children can test their predictions, moving the story props across the lake to safety. This will lead to a discussion of things that float and things that sink, and also to questions like "If we change the shape of the (object) will it still sink/float? What will happen to the sinkers/floaters if we change the amount of water that is in the water container?" These questions can be the basis of planning and conducting investigations.

Free play with floaters and sinkers

During free choice time let children play with a variety of objects that float and sink. Also have available materials out of which

SUGGESTED AUSTRALIAN SCIENCE PROFILE
OUTCOMES
The unit spans levels 1, 2, and 3 in the strand:

- Working Scientifically (Planning investigations;
  Conducting investigations; Processing data)

and levels 1 and 2 in the strands:

- Natural and Processed Materials (Structure
  and properties)
- Energy and Change (Transferring energy)

children can make boats and use the lake to test out the different boat models.

Planning and Interpreting Investigations

The storytelling session and the free-play activity should stimulate children to ask questions that reveal their understanding and suggest investigations. Record their questions on chart paper.

Help the children develop and refine their questions. Encourage them by asking questions that:

- Suggest things to investigate: What would you like to know? (Does the depth of water make any difference to whether an object floats?)
- Guide the process: What do we do? (How can we test this? What do we do first?)
- Interpret and evaluate questions: What does this mean? (What have we found out? How can we explain this? Where else have we seen things like this?)

Children's questions can prompt immediate investigations or be used as a basis for whole-group planning. Through their discussions during these investigations, children share their observations and interpretations, see what other children think, and

learn to work together as well as plan their investigations.

Some questions children may want to investigate:

Wood is heavy, so why does it float?

Why does a metal ship float?

Why do some light things sink and some heavy things float?

Why do both long sticks and short sticks float?

Why does playdough sink when it is shaped into a ball and float when it is shaped like a boat?

If the water is deeper, do more things float?

Suggested activities

- Sort objects and materials that float and sink.
- Make clay boats that will carry bigger and bigger cargoes.
- See how deep a boat floats in the water as its load increases.
- Design ways to make heavy objects float and light ones sink.
- See whether water depth makes a difference.
- Make different kinds of boats.
- Push a ball or balloon under the water and watch it "pop out."

Linking Home and School

Colin augments the experiences he has organized by sending home a small activity book on water. In the booklet, he encourages the children to find things around the house and see whether they float or sank in their bathtub (see Figure 1). The booklet contains a special page for drawing floaters and another for sinkers. Children bring the booklets back for individual discussions with Colin and for whole-group discussions.

What Have We Learned?: Who Sank the Boat?

Retell the story of "The Day of the Storm" using a couple of different boats and various sets of animals. Have the children again discuss who sank the boat and defend their judgments with ideas from their investigations. Bringing together some of the factors involved in floating and sinking, they should realize that it does not matter who jumped in the boat last, it is the total weight of all of the animals that causes the boat to sink.

Colin's Reflections

The children responded best to activities such as classifying objects into floaters and sinkers, looking at the materials, re-modeling clay to make it float and carry more cargo, attaching sinkers to floaters, and so on. All the while they generated questions, experimented, and tested ideas.

The real strength of the unit is as a base for formulating questions, planning investigations, experimenting, interpreting, and evaluating their findings.

Trying to explain why something floats or sinks is difficult—certainly for four-year-olds, and for the older children too. There are so many variables and the concepts are difficult—weight, density, shape, volume, buoyancy, displacement of water, forces.

I found the best way forward was not through ideas of force but of density. Children often seemed to have an intuitive sense of density (even though they got it mixed up with weight, volume, area, thickness). They seemed to use it to explain how different-size pieces of styrofoam all float; rocks all sink, regardless of their size; some kinds of wood float deeper in the water than others. From there we moved to a sense of "average density" by investigating mixtures of low-density and high-density objects, tying floaters to sinkers, taking account of the air inside a ball as well as its rubber shell, and so on.

Date:_____
*Find some things in your kitchen made from plastic, metal and wood. Which ones do you think will float?

Which ones do you think will sink?

Try them out in the bath or a bucket. Draw them on the next page...

Figure 1: A take-home sheet, for parents and children to work on together

Having said that, we still needed ideas of force: the water does something that makes things float (i.e., holds them up), their weight makes them sink, and the two forces are in competition. All pretty difficult really.

In fact most of the children were content with particular findings, answers to their particular questions, and not too concerned that their findings stopped short of a full explanation.

What Causes Floating and Sinking?

Principles of floating and sinking involve properties of the object (its weight, volume, density/average density) and the water (volume displaced, density). All of these concepts individually are difficult enough, but to understand floating and sinking, they have to be considered together.

Figure 2: A boat with a bigger load floats deeper in the water, displacing more water

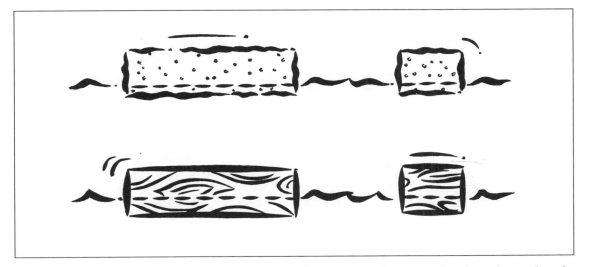

Figure 3: A big piece of styrofoam floats at the same depth as a small piece; timber floats deeper than the styrofoam because its density is greater

Objects don't float "on" the water, but partly in it. An additional weight makes the object float a little deeper (When it is totally submerged, no further adjustment is possible, and it sinks to the bottom.) When an object is floating, the water pushes up (the buoyancy force); its weight pulls down. The two forces are equal and the object sits there.

The buoyancy force depends on the amount of water displaced by the floating object: the deeper the object floats in the water, the more water it displaces, and the bigger the buoyancy force. The density of the water is important too—a boat floats higher in salt water (higher density) than fresh water. It is not simply the volume of displaced water that determines the buoyancy force, but its weight.

Oh No, Quickie the Cat Dissolved!

This unit is the third in a series of three that focus on water. Through a storytelling session involving the dissolving of the central character (Quickie the Cat, made from drinking chocolate), the concept of dissolving is presented. Children explore the idea and talk about the changes they observe.

Getting Started: The Story of Quickie the Cat

Find out what your children understand about dissolving by telling the story of Quickie the Cat. You can make Quickie from soluble drinking chocolate, dampened just enough so that it sticks together, then allow it to dry. Alternatively, simply wrap the powder in plastic wrap. Sugar or salt would also work, but not as well because children can't "see" them after they dissolve the way they can with the chocolate.

Jane tells the story this way:

JANE: One day, in a house, a little bit like your house, there was a pussycat. He was a very sleepy pussycat and he was always hungry and he was a little bit lazy and he always liked getting up to mischief. One morning when he was asleep the sun shone down and woke him up.

QUICKIE: Meow! Meow!

JANE: His name is Quickie, because he is made out of chocolate Quik™.

QUICKIE: Meow! Meow! Is anybody home? I'm really hungry.

JANE: Poor Quickie woke up and there was nobody home in the house. He was very hungry. There was nothing left out for him to eat!

QUICKIE: I'm so hungry and there is no food! Can you help me?

Materials

- Powdered drinking chocolate from which to make Quickie the Cat.
- Spoon with a face painted on: Spoonie.
- Materials that dissolve: instant coffee, drinking chocolate, sugar, salt, soap powder.
- Materials that don't dissolve: pepper grounds, rice grains, peas, oil, butter.
- Kitchen strainers—fine and coarse.

Unit Outline

DAY	WHOLE GROUP ONE	INTRODUCED EXPERIENCES	WHOLE GROUP TWO
1	Tell the story of Quickie the Cat, perhaps using puppets. Discuss what happened to Quickie as a means of finding out the children's understanding of dissolving.	Try to dissolve sugar, flour, oil, soap powder, coffee, and drinking chocolate into water. Have each child draw pictures of the things that dissolve.	Using their drawings, the children report back to the whole group about their understanding of things that dissolve and things that do not dissolve.
2	Have the children retell the story of Quickie the Cat. Can we get Quickie back?	Try reclaiming Quickie by straining the water, cooling the water, and evaporating the water.	Discuss how dissolving is different from mixing or melting. Is dissolving reversible?

CHILDREN: Yes. We can give you some cat food!

JANE: In another part of the room, Spoonie popped out because she heard Quickie meowing.

SPOONIE: Hello. Quickie is that you?

QUICKIE: Spoonie, Spoonie is that you? Are you home?

SPOONIE: Yes, we are the only ones home. All the others have gone away for the weekend and they have forgotten to leave something out for us.

QUICKIE: I am so hungry! Can you help me find some food?

SPOONIE: Maybe we could go into the kitchen.

QUICKIE: Let's go!

JANE: So off they went into the kitchen.

QUICKIE: Oh look, some sugar. I think I would like to try some of that.

JANE: Then Quickie jumped right in and started eating.

QUICKIE: Oh yuk! I think that is a bit sweet for me.

SPOONIE: You should only put your tongue in first to try it out. Oh look here is some flour. Maybe you would like to try some of that!

JANE: Instead of just tasting it with his tongue, Quickie jumped right in!

QUICKIE: Oh I don't like that! It is a bit dry.

SPOONIE: Quickie, you only need to take a tiny bit!

JANE: While Quickie was looking around, he found something else. It was salt. Do you think he would like salt?

CHILDREN: No!

QUICKIE: Oh yuk! Oh that hurts my tongue.

SPOONIE: I told you not to jump in. Just taste it with your tongue first!

JANE: Finally Quickie found a bowl of water. He decided to just take small sips. Spoonie was quite pleased that Quickie had finally taken her advice.

QUICKIE: Slurp, slurp . . .

JANE: But Quickie could not quite reach the water. So he tried to get a little closer.

SUGGESTED AUSTRALIAN SCIENCE PROFILE OUTCOMES
The unit spans levels 1 and 2 in the strands:

• Natural and processed materials (Reactions and change; Structure and properties)
• Working scientifically (Conducting investigations; Processing data)

Figure 1: Ben's cartoon of the story "Quickie the Cat"

QUICKIE:	Slurp, slurp . . .	JANE:	What happened in the water?
JANE:	Still Quickie could not quite reach. He made one last try but stretched too far and fell in. (*He falls into the water and dissolves*)	SAM:	The chocolate went right in and then he drank. He was drunk.
		SAM:	He broke.
QUICKIE:	Help, Spoonie! Help! Help, Spoonie!	JANE:	He broke. But why isn't he just sitting in the bottom of the water?
JANE:	Spoonie dived in to try and help Quickie. (*Spoonie dives in and out, mixing the chocolate into the water*)	SAM:	He soaked into the water.
		LOU:	Yeah, because you didn't hold on to him!
SPOONIE:	Where are you, Quickie?	JANE:	But how did he soak into the water?
LOU:	He's broken! He's broken off!	SAM:	When he jumped in.
SPOONIE:	Where's Quickie gone?	LOU:	It ruined him. It ruined the cat named Quickie! It's chocolate water!
SAM:	He broke.		
SPOONIE:	I will dive in and try and get you. Is that you, Quickie?	JANE:	How?
LOU:	No. He soaked, um . . .	LOU:	My mom told me!
RIKA:	No.	SAM:	The chocolate went into the water.
		RIKA:	Water makes chocolate melt!

Activities

Which substances dissolve?

Jane discusses with the group the idea of dissolving. She attaches a picture of Quickie the Cat and the chocolate Quik™ label to a chart she has made, headed "Things that dissolve." The chart is next to a range of materials for children to try dissolving into water.

These activities involved experimenting with common substances to see if they dissolved. The children categorized the substances and placed them on the chart, drawing pictures of things that dissolve and things that do not dissolve. The children enjoyed the activities. Many became frustrated when the oil wouldn't dissolve! They insisted on trying another substance until they found something that did dissolve.

Where did Quickie go?

Children saw that Quickie becomes spread throughout the water. As well, the total volume of the mixture (chocolate plus water) is barely different from the volume of water alone—Quickie goes "in amongst" the water. They found the same thing for other substances they dissolved.

For a few of the children, the idea that Quickie when he dissolved somehow no longer took up space was an interesting issue: how could he still "be" if he no longer took up space? I talked to the children briefly about the idea that Quickie must have gone into spaces inside the water.

Getting Quickie back

The children had earlier done the unit "The Scientific Birthday Party," where we looked at melting and freezing and so on and saw that we could get liquid water back by melting ice or condensing steam. I asked them "Is there any way we can get Quickie back?" They were confident that we would not be able to get Quickie back "whole," because, they said, pointing to the color of the water, he was "all over the place." However, we might be able to get the chocolate back and rebuild Quickie.

We talked about different ways we could try. If Quickie were made of peas or rice or sand, we could get him back by pouring the mixture through a strainer, or letting the mixture stand for a long time. If Quickie had melted, we could get him back by freezing the mixture in the refrigerator. But it was hard for the children to shift attention from Quickie to the water, and suggest that we boil away the water to see if Quickie was left behind.

We tried these different methods, and talked about how dissolving was different from melting and different too from just being in a mixture.

Linking Home and School

The children also did activities with their families at home and recorded the results in their activity books. Figures 2 and 3 show a few examples.

Date: 1 - 8 - 93

*Draw what you know about the water cycle...

Write about it:
The rain comes from the clouds.
Sometimes the sun dries the
water up.

Date: 3 - 8 - 93

*Look at the mirror or window in
the bathroom after someone has had
a hot shower or bath.
Draw what you see:

Write what you see: It goes all foggy
                    and you can draw
                    on it!

Draw

Date: 4 - 8 - 93

*Find something (with Mum or Dad)
that you think might dissolve.
Draw it:
        Sugar will dissolve.

Stir it in water....what happened?
It dissolved when I stirred it
with a spoon.
The sugar sort of goes away!

Figure 2

Date: 6-8-93

*Find some things in your kitchen made from plastic, metal and wood. Which ones do you think will float?

The plastic bowl because it's light and looks like a boat!

Which ones do you think will sink?

The wooden spoon and the sieve
The icecream scoop will ✗ sink because it's heavy.
The rolling pin will sink because it's wood.
It will sink (mixer) It's heavy.

Try them out in the bath or a bucket.
Draw them on the next page...

Floaters

Rolling pin
 Wooden spoon

Plastic icecream scoop

Plastic bowl

Sinkers

Metal mixer

Metal sieve

Date: 7-8-93

*Choose something else that you think might dissolve.

Draw it:
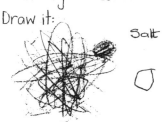 Salt

What happens when you stir it in water?

It dissolves and makes the water taste salty (and yummy!)

Parents- Extra Suggestions (if you're keen!)

* Dissolve some sugar in a small glass or jar of water until the solution is saturated (no more sugar can dissolve).
•Tie a piece of string around a paddle pop stick.
•Wet the string, then sit the pop stick across the top of the jar so that the string hangs in the solution.
•Mark the water level on the side of the jar. Put it in a warm place and watch what happens (this may take a week or two!)

* Find a puddle on some concrete near your house (preferably exposed to the sun).
•Draw around the edge of the puddle with chalk.
•Check the puddle at regular intervals...
...what's happening to the puddle of water?

Have fun, Cathy ☺

Figure 3

How Do You Make Hard Vegetables Soft?

"How do you make hard vegetables soft?" asked Joe. "With heat, of course!" Zinta replied. "What do you mean, heat?" said Joe. Zinta put Joe's hand on a heater.

Many children are not familiar with the word *heat* and find it confusing. Indeed, adults use the word in different ways, sometimes as a noun, sometimes as a verb, often loosely.

On the other hand, children are quite comfortable with the term *hot*, by which they usually mean high temperature. And they are often at ease with *heat* as a verb (Let's heat this milk on the stove") and the idea of a *heater*.

In fact children's preferences are consistent with scientific uses of the term. Heating is a process, a way of transferring energy—the energy flow that occurs naturally from an object at high temperature to another at lower temperature. It is best in science to avoid using *heat* as a noun—use *energy* instead.

In this unit Lee describes how he helped a group of young children refine their understanding of heating. He concentrates on everyday situations, like cooking, room heaters, and keeping warm.

Getting Started: Setting the Agenda

Introductory activities

- Turn on all the heaters in the classroom. Ask the children to explore things that are hot and cold in the

Materials

- Stove and refrigerator (with freezer).
- Large ice-cream containers, plastic cups, warm water, cold water.
- Thermometers.
- Objects to add to hot and cold water—marbles, spoons, stones.
- Jello crystals.
- Hot-water bottles (or plastic soft drink bottles) and towels to wrap them in.
- Fabrics with different insulation properties.
- Magnifying glasses to examine fabrics.
- Hot plate and Pyrex saucepan or electric fry pan.
- Vegetables.
- Materials to make a small fire (outside and safely).

Unit Outline

After an opening discussion and exploration of hot and cold, children develop a set of questions they would like to answer. They do activities that address their questions, then bring ideas together as they reflect on what they have done and learned.

GETTING STARTED: SETTING THE AGENDA
• Discussion and concept map
• Exploring hot and cold
• Asking questions

INVESTIGATIONS: ANSWERING THE CHILDREN'S QUESTIONS
• How do you turn something hot into something cold?
• How do you make a hot-water bottle hot?
• Why is the sun hot?
• How come clothes in winter make us so hot?
• Why do hard vegetables become soft in hot water?
• How come a fire is so hot and can burn you?
• If water comes out of a tap, how come some is cold and some is hot?

BRINGING IT TOGETHER: ENERGY AND US
LEE'S REFLECTIONS

SUGGESTED AUSTRALIAN SCIENCE PROFILE OUTCOMES:
The unit spans levels 1 and 2 in the strands:
• Energy and Change (Energy and us; Transferring energy; Energy sources and receivers)
• Natural and processed materials (Structure and properties; Reactions and change)
• Working scientifically (Planning investigations; Conducting investigations; Processing data; Evaluating findings; Using science)

room and things that are used for heating.
• Talk with the children about winter and cold nights and mornings and how they affect us.
• Read *The Sun Is Always Shining Somewhere*, by Allan Fowler (Chicago: Children's Press, 1991).
• Conduct small group discussions and then make a concept map on heating. Use a focus question like, What do we know about heating things? The concept map summarizes the children's existing ideas on the topic and looks at relationships between ideas.

Discussion and concept map

First, Lee tries mapping with the word *heat* as the central idea. Many children have difficulty responding; the word has little meaning for them. However, he resolves the impasse by changing the central idea to *heating things*. Now ideas flow smoothly, yielding the concept map in Figure 1.

Exploring hot and cold

Children explore things in the classroom that are hot or cold or are used for heating. They list things they can see and feel, such as heaters, a kettle, the hot-water tap. They read magazines in the craft area and cut out pictures for a collage about making things hot and keeping things warm.

Asking questions

After their exploratory activities, they meet in small groups (six to eight children) to discuss what they have found and to list questions. To guide them, Lee asks:

1. What would you like to find out about heating things?
2. What are some investigations or experiments you could do?

The children are used to framing questions and at ease with questioning. Initially their discussion focuses on, What things are hot? Next they share their answers in the large group and follow up particular issues by talk-

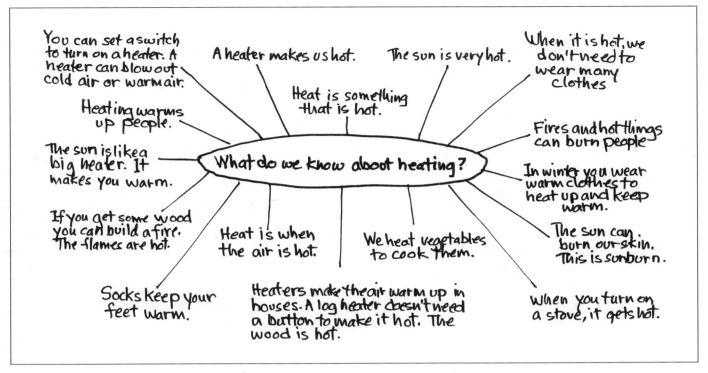

Figure 1: Concept map, What do we know about heating?

ing with Lee or looking in books. This puts them in a good position to formulate investigations in small groups. When all the questions have been assembled, sorted, and refined, they become the basis of the unit:

- How do you turn something hot into something cold?
- How do you make a hot-water bottle hot?
- Why is the sun hot?
- How come some clothes make us hot?
- Why do hard vegetables become soft in hot water?
- How come a fire is hot and can burn you?
- How come some tap water is hot and some is cold?

Now we had ideas and common interests to focus our topic and structure the unit. We sent a newsletter home to all families listing the children's questions. This enabled families to link in by sharing information and ideas and to help collect materials and resources.

Meanwhile, we started thinking about ways to answer our questions. First we made a list of possibilities: investigations, books, libraries, teachers, and people who know. One child offered a parent as an expert: "My dad is a plumber and he can tell us the answer." Ultimately we used all of these methods.

Investigations: Answering the Children's Questions

How do you turn something hot into something cold?

In a large group, children offer ideas and suggestions, methods like leaving things sit, pouring cold water over them, wrapping them in an ice pack, putting them in refrigerators. Lee teases out their ideas, asking, for example, where they have seen someone use a method like that, thereby linking ideas across different situations.

The group plans three experiments:

1. Making and setting jello.
   The hot dish is put into the freezer and the children time how long it

takes to cool down. Interestingly, only a small number know the name and role of a freezer (as opposed to a refrigerator). When talking about what happens as the jello cools, Lee introduces the language that *energy* has gone from the hot jello to the cold freezer.

2. Adding cold objects to hot water. Children add cold spoons, stones, and blocks to hot water and measure the temperature changes. Then they put the hot objects in cold water and measure that temperature change. (When adding a hot stone to cold water, it's best if there's only a small amount of cold water, in a plastic cup.) The children enjoy using the thermometers and comparing the thermometer readings with their own perceptions of how hot different things are. They tell stories to describe what happens when objects are added to water. As before, Lee encourages the language that *energy* went from the hot thing to the colder thing and that both changed temperature.

3. Mixing hot and cold water. Children mix hot and cold water in different proportions and measure the temperature changes. The children enjoy measuring the quantities, using thermometers and making predictions about how far the temperatures will change. A large amount of hot water contains more energy than a small amount of hot water. Temperatures determine which way the energy flows.

Lee focuses on the second and third investigations. He wants to draw out the following ideas:

• When a hot thing is near a cold thing, the hot one cools and the cold one warms.

• The hot thing and the cold thing eventually get to the same temperature, and the heating and cooling stop.

• We can think of something called *energy* passed from the hot thing to the cold thing as the temperatures change.

LEE:	Does it ever happen that you put a cold spoon in hot water and the spoon gets colder and the water gets hotter?
CHILDREN:	No!!
LEE:	If you put a hot rock beside a cold rock, would you ever see the hot rock cool down, way down, until it is much colder than the other rock?
CHILDREN:	No!!! That would be silly.
LEE:	What happens then?
JAMIE:	They come to be the same, then they stop.
LEE:	Which one of your experiments said that, Jamie?

Lee doesn't push the ideas too hard at this stage: there are other investigations to be done on the same theme. He is more concerned with introducing a language and a framework that the children can experiment with themselves.

Figure 2 is the concept map the children prepare while dealing with this question.

How do you make a hot-water bottle hot?

Even though the question has come from the children, it proves quite difficult. Many do not know what a hot-water bottle is. Some have used hot-water bottles at night but are unaware of how they are prepared: "It doesn't get made, it's just there." They assume that it has hot water inside *because* it is a hot-water bottle.

In small groups, the children experiment with adding cold water, warm water, and hot water to hot-water bottles. Hotter water makes the bottle hotter.

Lee talks to them about what they are finding and the things they are trying. They fill a number of hot-water bottles with different quantities of the same-temperature water. They wrap the bottles in towels (to simulate a bed) and leave them to see which ones stay hot longer. The children predict that the bottle with the most water will win and are pleased when they are right. Lee helps them link their finding back to the experiments with mixing hot and cold water.

Lee raises the idea that if you didn't have a "real" hot-water bottle, you could simply fill a soda bottle with hot water, screw the lid on tight and take that to bed. The children aren't so sure.

Why is the sun hot?
This is an exciting question. Numerous resource books and information on the sun are available and suitable for young children.

In a large-group discussion, all children are able to contribute information and knowledge about the sun. Many view the sun as a large ball of burning fire and try drawing pictures to capture what they mean:

The sun really is a burning fire.
The sun is a fire ball with fire burning all over it and shooting into space.

The sun is so hot because it really is a big ball of fire.
The sun is boiling fire all the time.

The children's investigations relating to the sun overflow into art, drawings, puzzles, and storybooks. Pictures of the sun prompt further questions relating to size, distance, what the sun is made of, and possible life forms.

Lee asks the children to imagine what our lives would be like without the sun. The children's main concerns are the loss of light and the loss of warming rays for themselves and other animals.

Lee likens the sun to sitting near a campfire, drawing on the idea that the hot fire gives energy to cold things around it.

How come some clothes make us so hot?
Initial investigations focus on the clothes the children wear to school. They make a graph of clothes they wear to keep them warm. The majority of children link warmth to wool:

Some clothes have wool inside them. It is called lining.
Socks can be made out of wool. This keeps your feet warm.

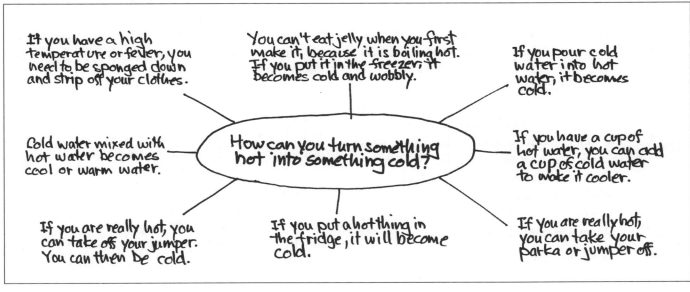

Figure 2

Clothes made out of wool can make us hot. Wool is thick and that is why dresses are so thick and hot.

This leads to further questions and explorations with various types of fabrics. Children examine various fabrics with magnifying glasses, wrapping hands in various fabric pieces, sorting by texture, comparing thickness, and observing clothes they are wearing.

Lee picks up on the belief some of the children have that clothes "make us hot." Do clothes make us hot the same way as standing near a fire makes us hot? Can we get hot by standing near a wool dress? The children try this. They also go back to the hot-water bottles, wrapping them in different materials to see which ones keep the bottle hot longer.

Lee talks with the children about the idea that clothes keep us warm by stopping our bodies from cooling down—stopping the flow of energy. Some children find these ideas straightforward and helpful, others put them aside.

Why do hard vegetables become soft in hot water?

A large-group discussion turns up no answers or possible solutions. The children first check the claim. They soak various vegetables in cold water at the same time as they cook some pieces in hot water (in an electric frying pan). The hot water makes a difference!

The children decide "to bring in an expert who knows the answer." The expert conducts an informal group discussion. Talking about favorite vegetables (and who hates spinach) and how vegetables are served gives the children guidance and ideas for further exploration.

After the visit, the children conduct more experiments with vegetables:

- Each child chooses a vegetable and observes, touches, cuts, and of course tastes. He or she looks through a

magnifying glass and sees vegetable cells and fibers. (What do they do with all the vegetables? Make vegetable soup of course!)
- Children place some of the soup vegetables in cold water only, and stir them a lot. It doesn't have the same effect as hot water.
- Children tape empty boxes together to represent the cells inside a vegetable. They then form a large circle and pretend to be water in a pot on the stove. As the water begins to "boil" the children jump around. While the water is "boiling," the children jump around on boxes, pummeling them. The boxes become slack and soft and fall apart. (A simple and fun activity, yet a powerful learning experience.)

How come a fire is hot and can burn you?

The children decide to make a fire (and a sausage sizzle) as part of their investigations. As children collect kindling and firewood they talk about safety issues, the difference in temperature at the top of the flame compared with the center, and blisters and burns. They discuss suitable types of wood for burning and appropriate distances to stand from fires. The children are content with their current knowledge of heat and fire, and want no more from the investigation than this social activity and the pleasure of the fire.

How come some tap water is cold and some is hot?

As with the hot-water bottle, the question shows how the child's world has so many things that seem simply to be there, in some mysterious way.

In Lee's class, Chris offers his father as a plumber and expert to help answer this question. In preparation for the visit, the children explore the kitchen and bathrooms. They turn on taps, feel water temperature, look at pipes under benches, and observe the color of taps. Chris's father talks to the children about where hot and cold water come from and how a hot-water heater works. He then leads the children on an exploration to trace pipes and find the school's hot-water heater. He tells the children how water goes into a tank and is heated up by an electrical element or gas fire under a tank. The hot water then goes through the pipes and waits for the hot water tap to be turned on. The children are encouraged to visualize the process. A child sums up the process this way: "It is the tank under the bench that heats up the water to make it hot."

Bringing It Together: Energy and Us

Lee and the children recall the activities they have done and the things they have found out. Then the children write a sentence and/or draw a picture about something they are pleased that they have learned.

All children are able to express some understanding of the concept of heating:

All fires are hot.

The thick clothes we wear in winter keep the energy in.

Water that comes out of the hot tap has been heated up by a gas fire and is hot.

Vegetables always become soft when boiled in hot water.

A hot stone doesn't go colder than the water it's in.

If you put more water in a hot-water bottle it lasts longer.

Lee's Reflections

The investigations on heat enabled all children to comprehend how important and essential heating and energy are in their daily lives. They were all happy with the ideas that energy flows from a hot object to a cold object until their temperatures are the same and that we can control the energy flow to some extent by things like blankets and clothes. There will be plenty of time for the children to refine and build their understanding later.

The Zoo in My Garden

Children are fascinated by living things. They pick up insects (dangerous or otherwise), chew on plants (poisonous or not), and revel in the dirt in the backyard. Many children are involved in their families' gardens. This interest provides a starting point for a unit exploring life and living things—especially plants and insects.

In this unit, children explore the garden together, observe things in it, make drawings, think about relationships, ask questions. In a natural habitat a wide variety of things live together in interrelationships suited to that situation. Even in a small garden, there are various habitats, with different physical and biological features.

The unit can be developed in different ways. In the account below, Maria explains how she went about the unit with a kindergarten/first-grade group. Tess outlines what she did with a second-/third-grade group. Maria focuses on animals, Tess on plants. Maria uses parts of the garden at school; Tess takes her group out each week to a garden near the school. Nevertheless, both teachers follow the same basic plan and address the same broad outcomes. They illustrate how the same basic structure and central ideas can be

developed at different levels and also how a second-/third-grade group can build on work done earlier in kindergarten or first grade.

Maria's Approach with Kindergarteners/First Graders

Getting started:
The school garden

- Draw a large map of the outdoor environment. Talk to the children as a whole group about their understanding of what could be living there.
- Ask children to identify features on the map that could be suitable habitats for various living things.
- Take children for a nature walk in the

Materials

- Containers in which to collect and house small animals (insects, millipedes, moths, snails, worms).
- Magnifying glasses.

We focused on animal life, acknowledging the critical place of plants but without going into details about them. This was simply to constrain the unit.

In the things they said during and after the nature walk, most children showed they already appreciated the complexity and interaction of living things in their local environment. Their knowledge of features, characteristics, names, habitats, and care requirements for creatures was considerable.

Collecting and caring for animals
The children collected things like aphids, snails, earthworms, butterflies, and even a kitten. We talked about how to look after the animals and were careful either to provide housing for the creatures we collected or return them to their natural setting within a few hours.

Studying individual animals
The children observed and identified characteristics by looking, touching, reading texts, and drawing on their previous knowledge. A record sheet (see Figure 1) helped them. They drew the animals, labeling and naming body parts and functions.

At the completion of individual work, children described to the whole group the various features of their animals. This was a beginning to comparing animals and thinking about diversity.

Similarities and differences
The children compared creatures, working from their record sheets and animals still available for observation. They put their observations on large charts, with headings from the record sheet like "Where did you find it?" "How does it move?" "What other things did you notice?" (see Figure 2). In this way, the children considered biodiversity not only of features, but also of needs and habitats.

What is a habitat?
The children listed habitats in their local environment where they might expect dif-

---

Unit Outline

GETTING STARTED
• Engaging the children
• Introducing the themes of habitat, features and needs of living things, relationships within a habitat, diversity of habitats

EXPLORING BIODIVERSITY
• Looking in detail at selected living things
• Pooling findings and identifying similarities and differences

COMPARING HABITATS
• Comparing the habitats in which living things survive

NEEDS AND RELATIONSHIPS
• Exploring the needs of living things, how they are met, and relationships within a habitat

ACTING RESPONSIBLY
• Reflecting on human influences and effects in a habitat

SUGGESTED AUSTRALIAN SCIENCE PROFILE OUTCOMES
The unit spans levels 1, 2, and 3 in the strands:
• Life and living (Living together; Structure and function; Biodiversity, change and continuity)
• Working scientifically (Planning investigations; Conducting investigations; Processing data; Evaluating findings; Acting responsibly)

---

area and record things they find. Allow them to collect some living things to bring inside for closer inspection.

The nature walk
For the nature walk, I gave children plenty of time to explore and browse. They took magnifying glasses, little spades, and containers. Indoors I set up a book and picture display on topics like earthworms, snails, butterflies, insects, life cycles, and lifetimes.

The animal I found _____

Where did you find it? _____

What does it look like? _____

What color is it? _____

How does it move? _____

What does it feel like? _____

What does it eat? _____

What other things did you notice? _____

What do you like most about the animal you found? _____

Figure 1: Record sheet

ferent collections of living things. I asked them to think of ones they thought would have lots of different things living there, and ones they thought would not have so many. The children made a rough list and talked about it briefly. For homework I asked them to keep an eye out for different habitats in the playground, on their way home, and in their gardens at home to think about which ones might have more things living there. The next day, the children revised their list. Part of their reasoning was based on direct experience. On the other hand, Anthea suggested she looked for places with lots of different plants and for places with healthy plants. There weren't any plants at all in the sandbox. Anthea's thinking raised the idea of interdependence of plants and animals.

Investigating particular habitats
The children selected two or three different places, some at school, some at home, and then studied them over a period of a week, keeping records of things they found (see Figure 3). I sent a note to parents, explaining what the children were doing and enlisting help. Each day, I held a brief reporting session where children could share their

findings. I encouraged children studying similar habitats to work together.

Thinking about needs, relationships, and responsibilities
From their work in the garden, children came to understand that all living things have needs for survival. The children closely examined their role in the world of living and began to question it. Louise noted, "We

WHERE DID YOU FIND IT?
Earthworms live in soil.
Aphids live on leaves in gardens and trees.

HOW DOES IT MOVE?
Cats run on four legs.
Earthworms move with bristles.
Aphids have tiny legs.
Snails don't have legs but they have a big foot.
People have two legs and two feet and can run.

WHAT OTHER THINGS DID YOU NOTICE?
Everything we found has a mouth.
Earthworms don't like light and snails don't like light.
Aphids like flowers and leaves and so do butterflies.

Figure 2: Comparing features, needs, and habitats

Figure 3: Habitats at home

really should not tread on and squash snails, because they are alive. I am alive and I don't want anyone to squash me, not even a giant."

Caring for living things

Children designed houses and living arrangements—specifically a "wormery" and a snail house—and cared for the creatures for a few weeks. They first researched the natural habitats and the needs of the creatures, then set up the wormeries and snail houses in fish tanks indoors. For the wormeries, the children collected soil, wet sand, composted leaves, et cetera, before finding worms. For snails, they collected fresh green leaves daily to place in the tank.

The demands of caring for the animals, imposed by the children themselves, promoted responsibility and led to an understanding of the complexity of dependence of living things on each other. The children were more inclined to take on responsibility for the care and survival of all living things in their school and home environment.

Maria's Reflections

Throughout the unit, the children practiced a variety of skills. They used observation skills to notice and represent details of the appearance of living things and habitats. This came through strongly in their drawings. They processed data by talking about their observations, individually with me or at whole-group time. Their investigations led them to answer questions and extend their knowledge and understanding.

Living things need food and water.

Living things can move and grow.

Living things indoors need to be cared for.

Living things are everywhere.

Everyone has a responsibility to look after and care for all living things.

One of the most powerful things they found out was how to act responsibly as they explored the outdoor area and how to care for the living things they found.

Tess's Approach with Second/Third Graders

My group of children investigated living things in a home garden near the school. I focused on levels 2 and 3 of the Science Profiles, knowing that some children were already at level 2 and most around level 1. I concentrated on:

- Features of plants, the diversity of plants, and the diversity of places in which plants live.

- Relationships that exist between living things, particularly the plants and animals in the garden we visited.
- Features of plants and the function of different parts of plants.

The basis of the unit was a series of weekly visits to a garden belonging to one of the parents. We focused on one garden over an extended period. In that garden, the children worked in pairs, adopting a particular space and observing it in detail from week to week. I wanted the children to concentrate on not just the features of the plants or animals they found, but how those features were useful in the plant's or animal's survival.

Getting started
Predicting: What living things might you find in a garden?
The children in groups of four brainstormed a list of plants and animals they would find in a garden. Their lists were long.

Some groups ran into trouble with definitions: what is "living," what is an "animal," what is a "plant"? I didn't want to get diverted too far into these questions—for example, we simply agreed that scientists think of insects, birds, worms, and so on as animals, just as we would. We did, however, take up the question of "alive/not alive." We started sorting things from the garden into these categories, but soon found we needed to add a third: "once alive."

Preliminary issue: Alive or not alive—Is soil alive?
We found ourselves debating the question, Is soil alive? Although this question was not the focus of the unit, it was one the children saw as important—we needed to resolve it before we could move on. As it turned out, the question was a valuable starting point, because soil is a mixture of the living, the never living and the once living—a habitat in its own right.

Children entered the debate with enthusiasm, from both sides. Discussion actually had to come to an end on one day but was enthusiastically continued the following morning. They were really working at clarifying their thinking and convincing the other side.

HEATHER: I reckon that soil is alive because animals go in it and make it alive.

TESS: How do you think animals make it alive?

HEATHER: Because they've got life in them, and, they give life to the soil.

TESS: How do they give life to the soil?

HEATHER: Well, they eat it and then they obviously go to the toilet and then that gives life.

TESS: Lauren, what's your idea?

LAUREN: Well I, my idea is pretty similar to Heather's. Um, I think bugs do live in it but they give all the nutrition to the um soil to give it to the plant, and, and the flowers and that.

TESS: So the soil gives the plants nutrients?

LAUREN: Yeah.

TESS: Does that make the soil living or not living?

LAUREN: Living.

TESS: Mathew, what's your idea?

MATHEW: I think that a rock could be alive.

TESS: Why?

MATHEW: Because like, um, rocks are made out of soil . . . like and the dead birds like they get buried in it and then they turn into a rock.

TESS: So a dead bird turns into rock and that makes the rock alive, does it?

MATHEW: No, um. Well kind of.

CHRIS : Has to be a live bird.

MATHEW: Well, there's, well, the bird's spirit is alive.

TESS: Does that make the rock alive or not alive?

MATHEW: Alive.

TESS: Okay. Who else has an idea, either way?

JILLIAN: Rocks and soil can't be alive because, well, they don't move and they don't breathe.

JULIANNE: I think ah rocks aren't alive because they don't breathe, there isn't any

mouth, they don't have anything to breathe with.

LUCINDA: Well, they're not alive. They just let plants and everything live because they eat and that doesn't make them alive.

TESS: Just because they help the plants to live doesn't make the soil alive. Is that what you're saying?

LUCINDA: Yeah.

Eventually we went out and got soil samples from different places in the garden and looked at them through magnifying glasses. The children were surprised at the mixture of things in some of the samples, especially the ones with a high component of compost. As it turned out both sides of the debate were satisfied that they were at least partially correct as we discovered that soil had an incredible number of living things within it as well as elements of nonliving and once living materials.

Exploring biodiversity, habitats, and relationships
The series of garden visits allowed the children to explore:

- The diversity of plants.
- Parts of plants and their functions.
- Habitats.
- Relationships between plants, animals, and the environment.
- The care a garden needs.

I used projects to give the children control of their work and a feeling for where it was headed. Their major project was a poster, produced in the sixth week, on some of their major findings. Smaller, weekly projects included:

- Making a map of the physical layout of the garden.
- Drawing a concept map of interrelationships in the garden.
- Preparing a poster on leaf litter and decomposition.
- Presenting a drama activity about insects.

Week-by-Week Activities and Management

WEEK 1
- Starter activity; unit planning.
- Visit garden (first visit): general exploration, children draw aerial views of the garden showing layout and different zones.
- In pairs, students select an area for long-term study and write detailed observations of plants, animals, and the physical features of their special area.
- Discuss garden design and the plants and animals in it.
- Initiate the class big book *How Does Your Garden Grow?*; start entering observations.

WEEK 2
- Language lesson on how to write scientific observations.
- Visit garden (second visit): children select plants for close study (structures, features, and changes over the next few weeks).
- Begin classifying plants (using chart); children select headings.
- Discuss plant similarities and differences, diversity, and classification.
- Record observations in class book.
- Drama activity: "Bugalugs."

WEEK 3
- Discuss needs and interrelationships in a garden: plants, insects, birds, worms, soil, water.
- Visit garden (third visit): teams look at relationships in their special area and observe chosen plants.
- Map relationships in a garden: parts of a garden listed on cards, relationships indicated with string between cards.
- Discuss needs and interrelationships of living things in a garden.
- Record comments in class big book.

WEEK 4
- Discuss parts of a flowering plant as a class; children draw diagrams (see Figure 4).
- Visit garden (fourth visit): Observe chosen plants, identifying parts and drawing detailed diagrams.
- Research names of plants in the garden and the conditions different plants prefer/need.
- Discuss compost, soil, and decomposition.
- Visit botanical gardens; study leaf litter, decomposition, relationships between plants, microbes, and small animals.
- Share information from excursion, posters, and drawings.

WEEK 5
- Discuss what is involved in keeping a garden and why such things are necessary.
- Visit garden (final visit): look at requirements of caring for a garden in context.
- Research "special relationships" in a garden (bees/flowers; worms/soil; microbes/compost; food chains; gardener/garden).
- Report on special relationships: drawings, enactments.

WEEK 6
- Reflect on what has been learned during the unit; further questions.
- Discuss and research selected questions.
- Children in groups plan and prepare posters on some of the things they have learned that they see as especially valuable, then present the posters to the class.
- Sum up the unit of work.

The children combined their direct experience in the garden with reading books, using charts and "keys" to identify plants, writing, drawing, and oral reporting, and visiting the botanical gardens.

Small-group work, whole-class discussions, and the drama activity helped bring ideas together. We also maintained a class book that we called *How Does Your Garden Grow?* where children from different groups recorded their observations and questions.

Tess's Reflections

Visiting a garden each week provided a rich, pleasant, and practical environment for studying living things. Just being in the garden inspired many questions that otherwise might never have arisen. It made the considerations of habitat, interrelationships, and the structure of plants relevant to the children in terms of both garden life and using books to further their knowledge. The children's understanding grew, and so did their confidence in talking about plants, insects, and garden life.

An afternoon in a garden each week was a very enjoyable way to spend time with the children! I was free to wander around, help them, and listen to their ideas. Overall, it was a refreshing way to teach and learn science.

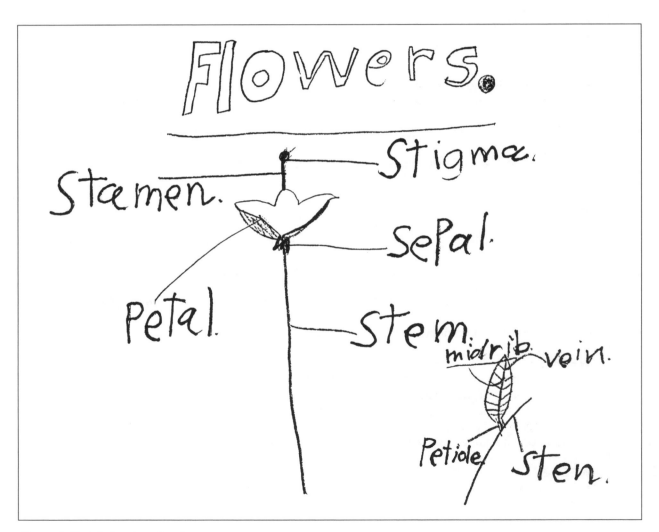

Figure 4: Craig's drawing of a plant

Pop Goes the Corn

Most children are familiar with popcorn. It is an interesting material to touch, taste, squeeze, make, share. In this unit children investigate the changes that corn seeds undergo in the popping process. Children learn to identify and describe the properties of the corn, use a range of senses and plan and conduct investigations. They recognize that changing the properties of a material can be useful (popcorn is more edible than corn seeds).

The unit is described by the teacher, Amy.

The topic can readily be extended into mathematics, environment, language, music, and art.

Getting Started

Past experiences with popcorn: concept map

The children talked about who had tasted popcorn, who had made popcorn, what it was like, where it came from, and so on. From their ideas, we constructed a group concept map (see Figure 1).

Buying corn: the supermarket and other shops

We walked to the local shops to buy some corn, checking out one student's suggestion that we could buy some at the video shop. We discovered that the video shop does sell popcorn, but it is already cooked, so we bought our popping corn at the supermarket. While we were there, we looked for other products that use corn. We took a collection of these back to school.

Materials

- Fresh popping corn.
- Hot plate and Pyrex saucepan, with small amount of oil (and/or microwave oven).
- Corn products to display on the interest table.
- Magnifying glasses.
- Small cardboard boxes or ice-cream containers to package eggs.
- Styrofoam pieces and popped corn for cushioning.
- Materials to make a scarecrow.

Unit Outline

GETTING STARTED
- Past experiences with popcorn: concept map
- Buying corn: the supermarket and other shops
- Interest table: things made of corn

POPPING THE CORN
- Preparing to pop
- Popping away
- Corn that won't pop
- What do we have now?
- Where did the water come from?

POPCORN FOR PACKAGING
- Dropping an egg
- Materials and their uses
- Parental input

EXTENSION: CORN IS A PLANT
- Where does the corn in the shop come from?
- Will popping corn grow if you plant it?

REFLECTION: WHAT HAVE WE LEARNED?

SUGGESTED AUSTRALIAN SCIENCE PROFILE OUTCOMES
The unit spans levels 1, 2, and 3 in the strands:

- Natural and Processed Materials (Materials and their uses; Structure and properties; Reactions and change)
- Working scientifically (Conducting investigations; Processing data; Using science; Acting responsibly)

Interest table: things made of corn

As well as the few things we had bought at the supermarket, the children brought from home items they could find made of corn. (I had sent home a note asking parents to help.) We ended up with a collection of boxes and tins of corn products (corn flakes, corn chips, taco shells, corn flour, corn soup, creamed baby corn). I put out fresh corn on the cob for the children to feel, a packet of corn seeds, and some reference books. Magnifying glasses and magnifying boxes containing corn seeds were also on the table. Children went to the interest table often throughout the unit, sometimes singly, often in pairs, examining the items.

Popping the Corn

Preparing to pop

The children examined the popping corn. As the children passed it around in cups, I asked naive questions like "I wonder what color you would call that seed?" and "Can anyone tell me how it feels? I haven't had a turn yet." The children described the seeds as hard and yellow. Jason volunteered "It's living," an idea we explored later.

I explained to the group the concept of "properties," and we listed properties of the corn seeds. Then we went on to corn flakes, corn flour, and fresh corn, looking at similarities and differences.

The children tried to predict how many cups of popped corn one cup of popping corn would make. Predictions ranged from one to eight, with one person suggesting 100. His contribution was valued too. It was pleasing to see the children actively anticipating and risk taking. We used paper to make a graph of responses on an easel. Making and recording predictions are important aspects of working in a scientific way.

Popping away

I asked the children what we needed to pop the corn, and what we had to do. The children had a number of different ideas: use the microwave oven, heat it in a saucepan, add some oil, don't add oil. Nobody wanted to immerse it in water.

We put together a plan for trying the different ways and comparing them. On the

MATHEMATICS
- Classifying things as hard and soft in small groups of five items: unpopped corn, popped corn, cotton balls, Styrofoam, wood.
- Estimate how many cups of popped corn will result from cooking the corn and how many corn seeds are in a jar.
- Explore concepts of space by asking children to put a packet of corn under, beside, and on top of the table.
- Provide a large container of corn seeds and measuring utensils for free play and at this activity volume and capacity were talked about (*full* and *empty*, for example).

ENVIRONMENT
- Discuss environmental aspects of popcorn.
- Leave some popcorn and some Styrofoam out in the garden to see which is biodegradable.

LANGUAGE
- Have reference books available for the children to look at and discuss.
- Dramatize the story of *Not Now, Said the Cow*, giving all the children the chance to actively participate.
- Learn the finger plays *The Scarecrow* and *The Earthworm*.
- Have children draw aspects of seeds and their growth as a prereading and prewriting exercise.

ART
- Let children paint soil and corn seeds and other interpretations of the topic.
- Trace and cut out five corn templates and sequence them in order of size.
- Make a scarecrow.
- Make a frieze of the animals in the story *Not Now, Said the Cow*.
- Let children form their name out of corn seeds and glue the letters to a strip of wood.

MUSIC
- Use music to underscore aspects of the topic (for example, the corn seed growing in the soil, the rain coming down, the sun shining).
- Use the audiotape *Popcorn* to accompany creative movement and exercises.
- Learn songs related to the topic (for example, "Corn, Peas, Beans, and Barley Grow" and "The Farmer in the Dell").

Table 1: **Extending the topic across the curriculum**

hot plate, we heated the corn in a glass cooker, so everyone could see the changes. Even with the microwave, children could see through the door.

Watching the pot on the hot plate, Rebecca commented on the water on the inside of the lid. I removed the cover briefly so everyone could see the steam rising and the vapor condensing. There was much excitement when the corn popped. They used their words to describe it all, and I took the opportunity to introduce scientific vocabulary: steam, water vapor, pressure, expanding. I made analogies with expansion by using a balloon.

Investigations don't always run smoothly. With another group of children, I used a different packet of popcorn. When the corn failed to expand, I suggested that I should buy a new packet at the shops and we'd try again. We discussed how sometimes things don't always go as you expect, and the first thing to do is try again. This was an important message about working scientifically; we often need to repeat experiments before coming to definite

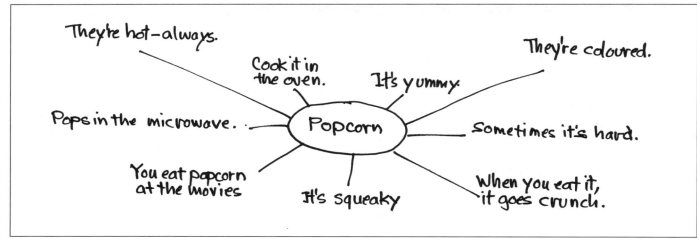

Figure 1: Group concept map: popcorn

conclusions. It also raised for investigation the question "Why didn't the corn pop?"

What do we have now?

Now that the corn had popped, we could compare our predictions about volume with what actually happened. One cup of corn had made about nine cups of popcorn! I could see that this was becoming a valuable math experience too!

The children compared the corn before and after popping. The popped corn was white and soft whereas previously it had been yellow and hard. Everyone wanted to eat it now. Before, "Only the birds would."

By changing the properties of natural materials, we can make them more usable. We talked about this idea more generally: look at corn flakes, corn chips, corn flour, corn soup, fresh corn. We looked up some books and pamphlets on how foods are processed and talked about why they were processed in particular ways.

Where did the water come from?

The children had observed the steam and the condensed water on the lid during the popping. Where did the water come from? Was it important in the popping? To demonstrate how an individual seed explodes,

I used a candle and heated a very small amount of oil in a test tube (you can also use an electric frying pan). As soon as the oil started to smoke, I added two or three seeds. The children, gathered around in small groups, could see the water on the top of the tube and the violence of the seed's explosion.

Help students make links between the steam, the explosion, and the changes in the corn. Draw their attention to the split in the popped corn: the heating evaporates the water inside, and eventually the steam pressure builds up until it splits the outer skin, with a sudden release of the steam. The children may notice that some of the corn seeds have not expanded and their skins are not split.

The heating, steam formation, and trapped steam inside the corn's skin are the critical aspects of the process. If the corn has dried out, it won't pop; if the skin has softened (so that steam is able to escape as it forms), it won't pop.

Corn that won't pop

Conduct some investigations into why "stale" corn won't pop. Investigate what happens when the seeds are dried before trying to pop them and when they are soaked for brief periods and long periods. These activities provide good opportunities for children to design experiments and "fair tests."

Children can also investigate popping balloons: as with the corn, the pressure inside can become so great that the "skin" splits.

Popcorn for Packaging

Corn becomes soft and fluffy when it is popped, reminiscent of Styrofoam chips. Is popcorn useful for packaging? When I asked the children whether an egg packed in popcorn would break, they chorused yes. We proceeded to test the prediction.

Dropping an egg

I provided each working group with a small box, popped corn, Styrofoam, and three eggs. Each group carried out the following investigations, after the class as a whole had agreed how we should do the investigation to get a meaningful result.

- Children packed an egg in Styrofoam in the box. Some children thought it would break when it was dropped. (We had previously discussed how fragile and breakable items such as televisions, plates, and computers are and that they are packed in Styrofoam to prevent their breaking.) Each child in a group had a turn at dropping the packaged egg. It didn't break!
- This time popped corn was used instead of Styrofoam to package the egg. Again everyone had a turn at dropping the egg. Result: the egg unbroken, and much disbelief among the children!
- An egg was placed in the box with no packaging at all. On the first drop it broke—to much hilarity.

I used a story to reinforce the ideas. Goldilocks wanted to send Baby Bear a mug for his birthday but she couldn't think of a way to keep it from breaking in the mail. Luckily she had a friend, Striped Frog, who suggested that she pack it in popcorn. Baby Bear loved the mug and it wasn't broken. The children dramatized the story the next day.

Materials and their uses

We talked about reasons for using Styrofoam rather than popcorn and popcorn rather than Styrofoam. Popcorn is edible (for mice as well as people) but popcorn has the advantage of being biodegradable.

Through this activity children were learning that science can be used to help us—in this case, by protecting objects from breakage. They were also discovering another example of the value of changing the properties of a substance. Not only was popcorn now edible, but it could help us transport things safely, and did not create difficulties of pollution.

Parental input

Through the class newsletter we kept parents informed about our investigations. One mother sent me a newspaper article she had seen on a new form of packaging. It looks exactly like Styrofoam but is actually made of corn starch and is completely biodegradable! It is now being used by some major information technology companies to protect their products. I was able to share this new knowledge contributed by a parent with the children. It was a good example of humans acting responsibly, using scientific knowledge to protect our environment.

Extension: Corn Is a Plant

Where does the corn in the store come from?

I asked this question, but no one had thought of this: the corn was just there! Again by my using naive questioning, we constructed a story: from farm to factory to store. I developed a number of activities, including dramatizing the corn growing and being harvested and transported to the warehouse for packaging. We made up songs, finger plays, and stories; we built a scarecrow outside, and some of our activities took place around it.

Will popping corn grow if you plant it?

We were able to build on Jason's early comment that the popping corn was living. I brought in pots of soil containing sandy loam, clay, and potting mix, which the children looked at, smelled, and touched at the interest table. We planted some unpopped corn in each kind of soil and some popped corn in three similar pots. It took a few weeks for the unpopped corn to shoot. The popped corn didn't. This raised interesting questions about whether the corn seeds were alive or not (can something dead give rise to something alive?), and the idea that heating had changed them to nonliving material.

Reflection: What Have We Learned?

It came time to ask children to recall and reflect on their investigations about popcorn. We drew on the activities we had done, and the informal time the children had spent with things on the interest table. Through naive questioning and subsequent discussion, I collected their ideas and put them together, as at the start of the unit, in a concept map (see Figure 2). I then brought out the original map for comparison. This

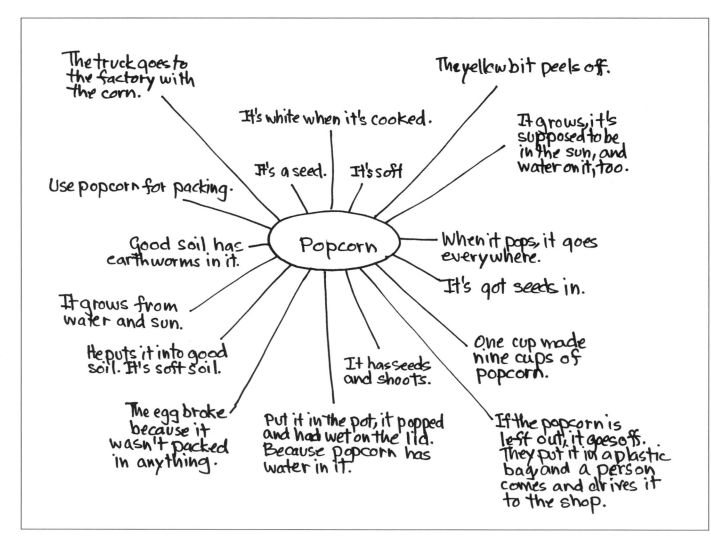

Figure 2: The revised concept map

was valuable, because it showed the children where they had come from: they enjoyed how much they had done and learned.

Amy's Reflections

Learning about natural and processed materials involves as a first step identifying materials, their uses and properties. The final concept map indicates that the children, as a group, were able to identify properties and changes that occurred in the corn. They commented on the uses of the new properties. Through the extension activities they also developed a broader understanding of corn's origins as a natural material and the ways materials are processed. Popping and investigating corn provided an effective context in which to improve their skills in working scientifically—both investigating and thinking about responsible uses of science. What's more, they enjoyed the topic!

My Special Flashlight

Children love to take flashlights under the bed sheets or to shine them outdoors at night. In this unit, children use flashlights as a way into thinking about electricity and light. The emphasis is on transferring energy—by mirrors, windows, shutters, and lenses for light; by wires and switches for electricity. The unit culminates in the children's designing a "special flashlight" of their own.

Getting Started: Experience with Flashlights

Joan wanted the opening session to engage the children's interest, give some indication of what they already knew, and set the direction for the unit, so she:

- Asked the children to bring in a special flashlight to show their fellow students.
- Read a story involving flashlights and invited the children to talk about their experiences with flashlights and the dark.

The children put the flashlights they brought in on a "special" table. Joan organized

Materials

- A large collection of flashlights (cheap and simple ones that children can dismantle), plus some special-purpose flashlights, including one with a clear plastic case.
- Batteries.
- Big cartons that children can climb inside to experience darkness.
- A bed sheet for a shadow-theatre screen, and a light source (an overhead projector, for example).
- Mirrors.
- Magnifying glasses.
- Some convex and concave lenses (e.g., glasses for farsighted and nearsighted people).
- Cardboard tubes (e.g., paper-roll holders, mailing tubes) to make light mazes.
- Sheets of cellophane and colored cards.
- Prisms.
- Flashlight raw materials: batteries, bulbs, connecting wire (with the ends bared and alligator clips attached), battery holders and light-bulb holders.
- Some switches or materials to make switches.

Unit Outline

DAY	WHOLE GROUP ONE	INTRODUCED EXPERIENCES	WHOLE GROUP TWO
1	Discuss: • People who use flashlights • Flashlights in stories • Personal experiences with flashlights Compare flashlights: • Shapes and sizes • Batteries • Brightness of light	Find out about flashlights in a darkened room or large carton. Play with light and shadows. Plan and prepare shadow plays and puppet shows.	Present shadow plays and puppet shows.
2	Plan investigations. Plan puppet show.	Experiment with flat mirrors, curved mirrors, windows, shutters, lenses, colored filters. Prepare for puppet shows.	Sum up what we have learned about flashlights. Present puppet show.
3	Discuss why we can't see in the dark and how the flashlight lets us.	Write a story about flashlights and the dark.	Read some of the children's stories.
4	Discuss how you think flashlights work. Draw pictures of the flashlight and its components.	Find out what actually is inside and how it actually works.	Report back: What did you find?
5	Plan how to make a flashlight if you just had some batteries, some wires and a light bulb.	Make a flashlight.	Discuss the need for a "closed circuit": what do you have to have for the bulb to light?
6	Think about how you might improve your flashlight (e.g., by adding a switch, a reflector, more light bulbs).	Improve the flashlight design. Alternative: Make a lighthouse.	Display models. Discuss how the switch works. What's inside a light bulb? What happens when you add more light bulbs?
7	Develop a group concept map of all of the things we know about flashlights and their light.	Draw a poster, showing a special flashlight; show its special uses and features, and how it would work.	Display and discuss posters and designs.

ness of their lights, features of their designs, and relationships between design and use. What was the key-ring flashlight for? Did it matter that it wasn't very bright? Who would use the waterproof flashlight? Which flashlight might be most suitable for a police officer? going camping?

Flashlights and shadows
Each child took a flashlight and began exploring its light. Joan drew drapes that darkened the room somewhat. She also had some big cartons, painted black inside, that two or three children could hop into. They explored shadows. They tried to shine the light around the corners of boxes and furniture and made clouds of chalk dust to show the beam in front of and beyond the corner.

Then the children, working in groups, planned and put on brief shadow plays, enjoying the illusions they could create. To make strong shadows, Joan used the overhead projector.

Controlling the beam of light
Joan put out a collection of objects the children could use to change the direction and the intensity of the light from the flashlights:

• Table 1: flat mirrors, curved make-up mirrors, shiny spoons, steel cans, cardboard tubes.
• Table 2: materials to use as "windows"—transparent, translucent, and opaque plastic; cellophane of different colors; office paper of different thickness; magnifying glasses; prisms.

Puppets set the scene
Joan introduced the segment by telling stories using different types of puppets—this one a flashlight, that one a mirror, and so on. The puppets asked each other questions about what they were and what they did and demonstrated their qualities to each other.

The children and Joan then listed questions and puzzles they might investigate:

twenty-five flashlights herself, on another table: many were cheap and simple so children could dismantle them; others included a waterproof one, a long-handled high-powered one, a tiny one that attached to a key ring, a lantern type that clipped directly onto a big battery. One had a clear plastic case through which the metal strips and inner workings were visible. She stocked up on batteries of different sizes and put them on the table too.

Stories about flashlights
The children described the flashlights they had brought and why they were special. Then Joan read a story about children exploring a cave and some of their adventures. The story prompted the students to talk about their own experiences with flashlights, the dark, and dark places. Some of their stories were related to the flashlights they had brought.

The group then discussed who used flashlights and for what purposes. The children suggested a wide variety of people, starting with mothers and fathers and campers, then people in particular jobs, like nurses, police and burglars, and finally almost anyone who needed a portable light or a "back-up" light, including astronauts and underwater divers.

The children compared the different flashlights on display, looking at the bright-

- How can we get the flashlight beam to go down one cardboard tube and back another?
- How can we use a flashlight to send messages?
- How can we make the flashlight beam into a small spot on the wall?
- Can we combine colored cellophane sheets so that no light comes through?
- What do we get if we shine two different-colored light beams onto the same spot on the wall? red light onto a piece of colored paper?
- What happens when we shine light through a prism?

Investigations

In pairs, the children began an investigation of their choosing—sometimes a puzzle, sometimes a question. Joan talked with them as they worked, helping with planning, ideas, and interpretations:

What would happen if. . . ?

How could you check that. . . ?

What have you found with. . . ?

Does this mean. . . ?

The children shared ideas and findings informally during their investigations. Pairs of children, one from "mirrors" and the other from "windows," came together formally from time to time, one from 'mirrors,' the other from 'windows,' to explain what they had found.

Puppet show: What have we learned about light?

Pairs of students put on brief puppet shows, like the one that Joan had given at the start, in which they used the puppets to explain what they had found—solutions to sending light around corners, the effects of shining light into a spoon or through a magnifying glass, what happens with colored filters and prisms. The children then made a list of things they had learned, and put the ideas together into a concept map (see Figure 1).

How does the flashlight let us see?

The activities that the children had done had all been about visible light—the behavior of a light beam on its way to or through an object. They had not talked about the role of the flashlight in how we actually see.

Joan asked the children to explain how it is that they could not see in the dark, no matter how hard they tried, but if they turned on the flashlight, they could see things in the flashlight beam.

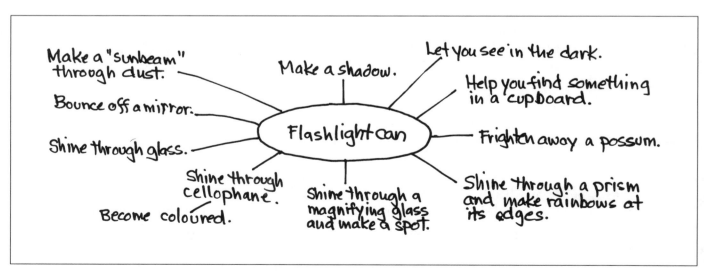

Figure 1: A class concept map on light

This was a hard question for the children: they wanted to say they saw because their eyes sent out light, like probing fingers, but they knew that wasn't right: if it were, they wouldn't need the flashlight.

Joan offered a further idea: if you shone two flashlights onto the pages of a big book to make two spots, what would you see if you put red cellophane over one flashlight? What if you now put red cellophane in front your eyes? The children offered predictions. Then they tried it—first with red, then green. Joan wanted to get to the idea that seeing depends on light coming into our eyes from something else, and that this light must be reflected from objects to our eyes.

The children were not sure. She tried a further demonstration. She shone a flashlight at the book, but with part of the page in shadow. Then she shone a second flashlight from a different direction, and the writing in the shadow became readable.

Joan asked them to identify the light source in situations where they could see—the sun, the room light, the car lights, a fire light, and so on. These were light sources, and their eyes were light receivers. The light beams traveled out from a source, bouncing off things in their path, sometimes being absorbed by objects on the way, and sometimes finding eyes to enter.

Summing Up with Stories

To complete the exploration of light, the children wrote stories about flashlights and seeing in the dark. Some wrote simple stories, recounting how they could see with a flashlight; others wrote about particular incidents and experiences; a few wrote fictional stories about losing the flashlight in the night or noises in the dark.

How do flashlights work?
Predict, explore, explain
Joan turned attention back to the flashlights on the table. There were many different designs, but how were all the flashlights the same? The children decided they all had a bulb, a reflector, a window in front of the bulb, a case, a switch, and batteries. They weren't so sure about handles—when is a handle a handle?

Predict: draw a flashlight showing how it works
Each child drew a flashlight, showing its parts and how she or he thought it worked. They then explained their drawings to each other. In many cases, they made little attempt to link the parts, they simply identified elements they felt were crucial. Everyone included the battery and the light bulb—the energy source and the energy receiver.

Explore: dismantling flashlights
To test their ideas, the children dismantled the flashlights. Most went first for the batteries, but once one child had opened the light-bulb end, others followed suit. Joan probed with questions:

> What happened when you turned on the switch?
>
> What were the metal strips and where did they go?
>
> What was the window for at the light-bulb end? What would happen if it were made of metal? red plastic?
>
> What was the metal shell behind the light for?

The flashlight with a clear plastic case enabled everyone to see how all the pieces fit together. But it was still difficult to see how the batteries actually made the light bulb light.

Explain: how does the flashlight work?
While the children were able to identify the key components of the flashlight—batteries, switch, light bulb—and understood that the battery was the energy source and the light bulb the receiver, many had no idea how the parts were connected (or even that they

needed to be). To address this issue, Joan invited the children to make their own flashlight (without a case). As a whole group, they brainstormed some possible ways to go. Jessica thought "you'd just sit the little light bulb on the battery and it would work, because the battery's got a lot of power." Tanya thought you'd need a wire, and you'd connect it to the light bulb. She was unsure about the connection, because she could see two possibilities—the point and the screw casing. She wasn't aware of the two terminals on the battery. Lieu was. He pointed out that one end of the battery was positive, and the other negative. But there weren't any labels on the light bulb. Armed with ideas like these, the children tried different ways of making the bulb light up. Some achieved it with a single wire (see Figure 2), some used two wires (see Figure 3).

Joan handed out light-bulb holders and battery holders to make it easier for the children to manipulate connections. As groups succeeded in making their bulbs light up,

Figure 3: Making the bulb light with two wires

they moved on to making "improvements," adding switches and reflectors and extra light bulbs. Some of the children used cardboard and Legos to make cases for their flashlights.

What have we learned about electricity?

Some of the children drew pictures on the blackboard showing how they had connected the pieces. Perhaps the major step forward for the class was their realization that the battery and light bulb had to be connected, so the electricity could get from one to the other. The wires enabled the transfer of energy. Switching the wires could stop the transfer, as could disconnecting a wire.

The children had various explanations of how the wires enabled energy transfer. Scott said there were electric currents. Elec-

Figure 2: Making the bulb light with one wire

tricity traveled out in both wires from the battery and clashed in the light bulb, causing light. (Scott is perhaps looking for a way to reconcile the idea of current flow with the idea of energy transfer.)

Bridget thought that the electricity traveled from the battery to the light bulb and back to the battery again. This is the accepted view, as long as "electricity" means the electric current. This is not true for energy: the energy doesn't come back. Electric current carries the energy out from the positive terminal, drops it in the light bulb (where it changes to light), and comes back "empty." So the current is like a convoy of trucks, taking energy out to the light bulb, dumping it, and returning.

Stephen couldn't see the need for the return wire. Perhaps he was thinking of electricity only as energy: the energy goes one way from the battery to the light bulb and is all dumped there. If "electric current" is something different from energy flow, what is it? What is actually flowing? (In fact, it is electric charge.)

These are difficult ideas. Children can't "see" electric current; they can't see what (if anything) flows. Nevertheless, they can be convinced that there has to be a return wire, and that a switch in one wire has the same effect as a switch in the other. The children tried this. They also looked through magnifying glasses at some of the light bulbs that had blown. They found that a blown light bulb has a break in the filament.

Armed with their new understanding, the children returned to the flashlights on the front table, looking for the connections. They drew pictures and explained what was happening (see Figures 4 and 5).

What about electricity in the house?

By this stage, the children had become very interested in electricity: Was electricity in their houses like the flashlight, with light bulbs and wires? They knew there were light bulbs, wires, and switches. They weren't sure about the source, but they knew it wasn't a battery.

JOAN: So how does electricity get to the power point?

GRACE: There are wires inside the walls.

JOAN: Where do the wires come from?

SALLY: From the pole.

JOAN: How does electricity get to the pole?

SALLY: From another pole.

GRACE: From one pole to another to another.

JOAN: Does it just go round and round and round from one pole to another and from one house to another?

ALL: Yes!

JOAN: But where is the electricity made? [Pause]

PAM: At the Electric Commission.

JOAN: Where does the Electric Commission get the power?

PETER: From the sun.

JOAN: How? I've never seen wires going to the sun!

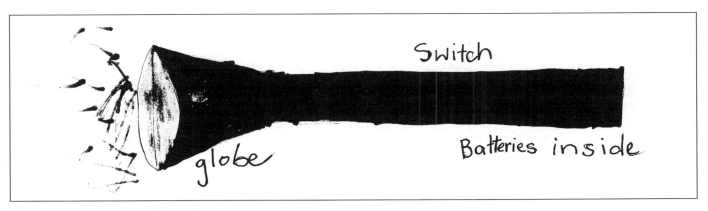

Figure 4: Explaining the flashlight (Lieu)

Why do torches need switches to switch them on?

Why do torches need batteries to work?

When you tarn the metal switch thing that throo through the buttree goes battery and the torche turnes turns on

Figure 5: How the switch works

PETER: A rocket goes to the sun and gets it.

JOAN: How?

PETER: A big tube gets it and puts it in the rocket.

ALICE: No, the tube would melt.

PETER: It's a special tube that doesn't melt. They put it in containers in the rocket, then it comes back and gives it to the Electric Commission.

GRACE: There's water so the tube doesn't melt. It keeps it cold so electricity can go into the rocket.

JOAN: Oh!

PETER: I think it comes from the moon.

JOAN: How?

GRACE: There's invisible pipes . . .

ALICE: And from the stars.

GRACE: When shooting stars come down they bring electricity and give it to the electric people.

PETER: No, stars just die and then there's nothing.

JOAN: So, electricity comes from the sun and moon and stars?

GRACE: And from rainbows.

Designing a "special flashlight"

To draw together ideas in the unit, the children contributed to a group concept map on the theme of flashlights. Part of the map focused on light control, another part was concerned with uses, and the final part dealt with electricity. Joan helped the

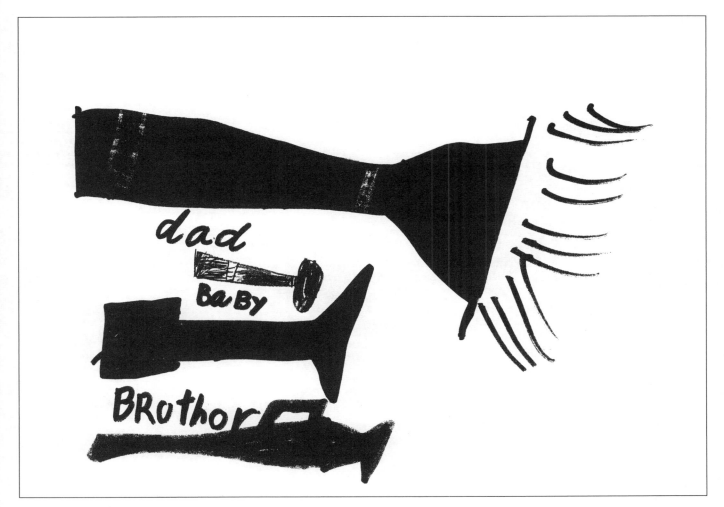

Figure 6: Kiri's special flashlights

students see parallels between light and electricity: one had light beams, the other wires; both had identifiable sources and receivers; both could be controlled during the transfer and by "turning off" the source.

Using these ideas as a springboard, each child designed his or her own special flashlight. Joan asked: "If you could have any flashlight, designed to do the things you wanted to do, what would it be like?" Some of their flashlights had special uses (to check on a pet at night, provide security) or special features (able to work in the bath, cast a red light, shine in two directions at once, stick on velcro, fit in a small pocket).

The children offered ideas to the group. Joan encouraged humor and outlandish ideas, and before long all the children were enjoying being clever about what they wanted. With this stimulus to guide them, each of the children decided on the special features they would like and then set about designing their flashlights.

They showed their designs on posters, somewhat like advertising posters, that pointed out special features and included an explanation of how their flashlight worked.

Mechanical Toys

Children and toys belong together. Children spend much of their time with toys—simple, complex, homemade, purchased—and are ingenious at working out what to do to make a toy move. But what happens to produce the motion? Finding out can help children learn about energy and appreciate toys in a different way. In this unit, they find out about transferring energy and the mechanisms and sequences involved. By exploring a variety of toys, they learn to identify energy sources and transfer mechanisms, including gears and electric circuits.

Children bring different values and knowledge to the study of toys, depending on their interests, environment, cultural background, gender, and so on. Teachers can build on and be sensitive to this richness by finding out about the different toys that children play with and the things that make those toys special.

Resources

You will need a collection of mechanical toys that use different energy sources (strings to pull, springs to wind, batteries, rubber bands, and so on). The toys need to be able to be dismantled easily and/or have mechanisms that are readily observed. Toys using wind-up mechanisms and gears are good because children can see the movement and the way energy is stored and transferred.

In addition to the toys you or the school provide, children can bring some of their favorites from home. Make it clear that it is their choice whether the toy will be dismantled as part of the unit.

You will also need simple materials like empty thread spools, rubber bands, drinking straws, cardboard, and popsicle sticks to construct a merry-go-round and other simple toys.

Materials

- A collection of suitable mechanical toys.
- Thread spools, rubber bands, popsicle sticks, drinking straws, clay, and cardboard to make the merry-go-round.
- Springs (for twisting, squashing, and stretching).
- A collection of batteries and electrical gadgets like motors, buzzers, light bulbs, and switches.

Unit Outline

RESOURCES

MAKING A START
• Wonderful toys that move
• My special toy
• Classifying toys by energy source
• Planning: children's questions
• Investigating: some principles of operation
• Springs that stretch
• Springs that twist
• Making simple toys

HOW DOES IT WORK? (WHOLE-CLASS
  INVESTIGATION)
• A strategy for finding out
• Energy transfers

HOW DOES IT WORK? (SMALL-GROUP
  INVESTIGATIONS)

HOW DOES IT WORK? (BATTERY-DRIVEN TOYS)
• Orientation: whole-group discussion
• Experimenting with circuits
• Investigating the frog
• Other battery-driven toys
• My special toy

WINDING UP THE UNIT
• Grouping the toys

SUGGESTED AUSTRALIAN SCIENCE PROFILE
OUTCOMES
The unit spans levels 1, 2, and 3 in the strands:

• Energy and change (Transferring energy;
Energy sources and receivers)
• Working scientifically (Planning investigations;
Conducting investigations; Processing data;
Evaluating findings)

Storybooks featuring toys could be placed on an interest table or read aloud during the unit.

Making a Start

Wonderful toys that move

Tracey's class began by listening to the song "The Marvelous Toy." Tracey asked them what the toy might be (a soldier? a robot? a monster?) and what might make it move (a battery? a computer? a spring?). The children offered ideas and acted out the movements in the song. This established the theme for the unit: toys that move and how they move.

The children chose toys from the toy box and set them moving. Tracey then directed everyone's attention to a battery-operated crab. What words could be used to describe its motion? Could the children imitate its motion? Could they suggest how and why it moved?

My special toy

The children brought a special toy from home—one that moved and one they wanted to show to the others in the class. Tracey explained that it would not be necessary to pull all of the toys apart—she set up one table for toys that were not to be pulled apart and another for toys that could be. Some children were unable to think of a suitable toy at home, so they chose one from the toy box.

The children, in groups of six, then showed their special toys, drew pictures of them and explained how they believed they moved.

Each group selected a toy or two to show to the whole class because the toy was unusual or because the children could easily see how it moved. Discussion focused on the similarities and differences.

Classifying toys by energy source

Tracey set hoops on the floor for sorting the toys into groups. The children suggested labels for the hoops, according to what made the toys move: *wind-up; strings; battery; spin.* They insisted on a further label, *don't know.* Each child placed a toy from the toy box or the tables into a labeled hoop saying why they had made their choice. Much discussion followed. This way of classifying objects was unusual for the children, because it was based on speculation about what was inside rather than on external features.

Tracey noted from the discussion that many children had begun to see that toys had chains of interactions—one part made another part move and so on. Energy was passed through the toy.

Planning: Children's questions

Tracey asked, "Do you have any questions about how any of these toys move?" The children put together a class list. Most started with "I want to know how ..." Tracey worked with the children to clarify and improve their questions, getting them to a form that made them researchable, and suggested a plan of action. Final questions included:

I want to know why, when you wind the crab up, it goes?

How does the spinning top work? When you pull up the handle and push it down, why does it spin?

How does the roller-skate doll move when you push the button? What makes the legs move?

I want to know how the chopper goes around.

The group didn't start trying to find answers immediately. First, they investigated the operation of some very simple toys and then tried making toys. They would come back to their questions when they had more ideas to work with.

Investigating: some principles of operation

Tracey wanted the children to understand toys as having related components through which energy is transferred and to find out about energy sources.

Springs that stretch

Children used accordion-folded paper to make a spring for a jack-in-the-box. It was springy, but not very strong. They made stretchy caterpillars from pipe cleaners wound around pencils. Once again, the spring was not very strong. How could they make stronger springs? They suggested using other materials—especially wire, metal, and rubber. Clay didn't make a good spring (they tried it!). They knew without trying that brick, wood, or cloth wouldn't either.

Tracey had some rubber bands of different thicknesses, as well as a number of metal springs, some made for stretching and some for compressing. The children played with the rubber bands and the springs, comparing them. They could see that compressed springs could make things move.

She introduced the idea of *energy*, by using a simple jack-in-the-box. The children gave energy to the spring by pressing it down. The lid kept the spring tight, but when they opened the latch, the puppet jumped up. The children were happy with the ideas that the puppet used energy to jump, that he got the energy from the spring, and that they had given the energy to the spring when they compressed it. The spring had held the energy, waiting, until the latch opened.

Springs that twist

The children examined some spiral springs taken from old toys; instead of stretching the spring, they tightened the coil. They made simpler ones from paper. They also made a variation on the spiral, twisting a rubber band and letting it untwist.

Making simple toys

The children made model merry-go-rounds from rubber bands and thread spools (see Figure 1). Tracey gave the children the materials and a picture of what she wanted them to make, and the children worked out how to make the toy. It proved to be a

Figure 1: **A homemade merry-go-round**

challenge. Tracey kept her own help to a minimum, asking questions like: "What does the merry-go-round need?" and "What does it need that for?" For example, the children said the merry-go-round had to have a motor and through elimination decided that the motor had to be the elastic band. Each child made his or her own model. They learned from each other and by trial and error, and eventually made the models beautifully with no problems in sequencing the parts. The materials included an empty thread spool, a popsicle stick, a toothpick, clay, cardboard, a rubber band, and a disc cut from a candle with a hole and slit in it.

The children experimented. What if they made the horse heavier? the bar longer? used a stronger rubber band? left off the clay base? How could they improve the design to make it go longer? faster? They compared their ideas and experiments, and drew pictures explaining the problems they had, and the improvements they invented.

How Does It Work? (Whole-Class Investigation)

A strategy for finding out

One of the questions the children posed earlier was "How does the wind-up handle make the crab's feet move?" Tracey's approach to answering the question was predict-explore-explain. Children were first to predict what happened inside the toy, then explore the toy (including dismantling it) to check their predictions, and finally, to write down their explanations. At each step, Tracey brought their ideas together on a large chart as a model for investigations the children would do shortly by themselves.

Energy transfers

To complete the activity, the children discussed the way energy is passed along in the toy:

- I turn the handle.
- The handle turns the gear wheel.
- The gear wheel turns the leg wheels. (As the teeth on the gear wheel turn one way, the teeth on the leg wheels turn the other way.)
- The leg wheels are not "full wheels": they are part of the legs and only move a little bit.
- I am the energy source—without me, the toy won't go. The crab's legs are the energy receiver—that is where the energy ends up.

Like the jack-in-the-box, the crab was a good choice for talking about energy. The children had some understanding of "personal energy", and the crab and jack-in-the-box fit with their experience: they used energy to move, and so did the jack-in-the-box and crab.

How Does It Work?
(Small-Group Investigations)

Using the procedure they used with the crab, the children, in groups of three, investigated how other toys in the toy box worked.

Tracey had selected the toys carefully. They included:

- A friction wind-up mouse that also involved some gears.
- A plastic monkey suspended on a plastic tree in a vertical cylinder of water that had a button at the base. Pushing the button created a water flow to spin the monkey.
- A wooden cut-out clown with pivot joints; its arms and legs were attached to strings that could be pulled.

WHAT WE THINK
The wind-up handle is like a motor.
There is a little machine thing inside it.

WHAT WE COULD DO TO FIND OUT
Just take off the top and look inside.
Read about toys in books.
Ask the person who made it.

WHAT WE DID
We watched the cogs turn the knobs that the legs hang on.
We looked in books and we found that wind-up toys often have gears.

WHAT WE FOUND OUT
The wind-up handle turns the gears.
As the gears unwind, the knobs [the teeth of the cogs] turn, and the legs, because they fit onto the knobs, move.

QUESTIONS THAT WE HAVE NOW
What if one of the knobs broke off?
What if the gears were bigger and had more knobs?

Figure 2: **How does the crab work? Predict, explore, explain**

The children completed worksheets (see Figure 3) using the same steps they had used earlier with the crab. Each group demonstrated and reported their findings to the rest of the class. The presentations helped children clarify their ideas and demonstrated different ways of investigating a problem. Tracey led them in comparing their approaches and discussing the ideas of energy source, energy receiver, and energy transfer.

How Does It Work?
(Battery-Driven Toys)

Battery-driven toys are more complicated, because the children cannot see what is happening in the battery, the wires, or motors. Tracey wanted to concentrate on the following ideas:

- The battery is an energy source (without it the toy won't function).
- The receiver can be a light bulb or a motor.
- Energy is carried from battery to energy receivers by wires (without the wires the toy won't function).
- The wires need to form a closed circuit, from the battery and back.
- A switch "breaks" the circuit, stopping the flow.
- A light bulb turns electrical energy into light; a motor turns electrical energy into movement.
- Energy can be transferred from the motor by gears and cogs.

Orientation: whole-group discussion
The children considered how a toy dinosaur with flashing eyes and a motorized roller-skate doll worked. They were able to suggest suitable circuits for the lights and postulate ways of making the eyes flash (by turning a switch on and off). They couldn't imagine how the electricity could operate such a switch. Some children suggested that the roller-skate doll must have a motor.

How come the monkey spins around by you just pressing a button?

What I think...
The bubels is full of ar
The bubels are poshing the monkey up The warter is pushing it up

Ways to find out...
Look inside / Look in a book /
pore the water out /
Tip the water out and See

What I did...
We pore the water out

What I found out...
The water is pusing The monky upso it moves

Questions I now have...

Figure 3: Amy and Adele explain how the monkey works. They connect the movement of water to the movement of the monkey (the receiver), but it is not clear that they see themselves as energy source, pushing the button to move the water.

Experimenting with circuits

The children experimented with motors, buzzers, switches, and light bulbs in circuits, clarifying ideas that the battery was the energy source, the wires enabled and guided the transfer, and the bulb, buzzer, and motor were receivers. Tracey provided some little motors with the cover removed, so the children could see how connecting the battery made the coils spin. They also looked inside a doorbell and saw that it too included a wire coil. Some of the children pursued these ideas and found out that electric motors involved magnetic effects. Most were happy with just knowing that a motor turned electrical energy into movement.

Investigating the frog

The children turned their attention to a battery-driven frog: "Why does turning the knob on the back of the frog make his arms and legs move?" They offered ideas: the knob was a switch; there must be a motor connected to gears. They took the frog apart and saw that they were right. There were lots of gears! They predicted which direction the various cogs would turn when the motor turned. It was hard to check, because they had to put the toy back together again to make it work, and then they couldn't see the cogs. However, their predictions extended to external parts, which they could check.

Other battery-driven toys

The children explored other battery-driven toys. However, they were confused when they dismantled the toys: they expected to see wires everywhere but often this turned out not to be the case. Tracey reminded them of their work with flashlights: there were not wires everywhere in the flashlight either. The batteries connected to metal strips, springs, and so on. The children then looked for these kinds of connections in the toys.

My special toy

Tracey asked each child to answer two questions about his or her special toy: *What* makes it move? *How* does it move? Some of the special toys could not be dismantled easily; others their owners didn't want to dismantle. This was therefore a time for conjecture, for testing from the outside what might be inside. Tracey encouraged alternative explanations, asking the children to think of different ways they could explain how the toy worked. The children worked in groups of four, looking at four different toys. This enabled them to develop different explanations and compare ideas. The groups reported on the options they had developed and the sequences of energy transfer involved.

Winding Up the Unit

Tracey compared the children's explanations of their favorite toys before and after the unit. Generally, the children were able to explain more fully how their toy moved, identify the source of energy, and explain how the energy was transferred. For example, consider Jack's and Adele's before and after comments:

JACK

(*before*) I pull a handle back and the bow and arrow shoots off. The handle makes the arrow go. (*after*) You pull back the handle and the arrow flies. When you pull the handle it tightens the string. When you let the arrow go the string comes back to where it was before and makes the arrow go.

ADELE

(*before*) It is Thomas the Tank Engine. How it goes. You press the button that says go and then it goes. It moves with batteries. I don't know how the batteries make it move. (*after*) It is Thomas the Tank Engine. It has a motor. You press the on button and if you press the off button it will stop. The on button is joined to a wire when it is on, and when it is off the wire has a break. The power is in the battery.

Grouping the toys

The children reconsidered their original groupings of the toys. Tracey noted that their justifications were more specific than at the start. When she asked them for a consensus about the groupings, debate was lively. The children decided that they wanted a "gears" group as well as groups based on energy sources. Tracey raised the idea that gears were a way of transferring energy, not an energy source, but to no avail. In the case of the frog, for example, they could not decide whether it belonged in the battery or the gears grouping, so they put its legs into the gear group and its stomach into the battery group! In their own way, they were identifying differences between a source of energy, the means of transferring the energy, and the energy receiver.

Making Dirt

Children enjoy playing in sand, water, dirt, and mud—building castles and mountains, making rivers and moats, looking for worms and crawling things, watching ants on the march, planting seeds. Their imaginations envisage another world underground, where rabbits, snakes, and crawling things live in tunnels and caves, congested networks of pipes dip into underground rivers, compost rots, and bones turn to dust.

Perhaps they don't see so clearly that soils are critically important to life on earth—and not just human life. Plants depend on soil; animals depend on plants; decay and decomposition depend largely on microorganisms in soil. Dust to dust, ashes to ashes. No wonder "the Land" is revered in so many cultures.

This unit is built around the idea of making soil—humans making soil, nature making soil. Children learn that soil is a mixture, that soils change over time. They think about how soils are formed—erosion, decomposition, and forces from inside the earth that cause mountains and volcanoes. They relate soil types to plant life and landscape. They see the capacity for human intervention in soil systems and realize that this intervention must be undertaken responsibly.

Getting Started: This Comes from That

Russell began by asking the children to track where things in their daily life had come from, to make the point of human dependence on the land.

RUSSELL: Let's try it. Joseph, what did you have for breakfast?

JOSEPH: Corn flakes and milk.

RUSSELL: Do you know where corn comes from?

JOSEPH: From the farm.

RUSSELL: And how is it made on the farm?

JOSEPH: IT GROWS, IN THE GROUND.

RUSSELL: What about the milk? Amy?

AMY: It comes from cows.

RUSSELL: And what do the cows eat?

AMY: Grass.

RUSSELL: And the grass grows in the ground. What is this door made from? Jonathon?

JONATHON: Wood.

RUSSELL: Where does the wood come from?

JONATHON: Trees.

RUSSELL: Where do trees come from?

JONATHON: They grow in the forest. . . .

Materials

- Large containers and trowels for collecting soil.
- Planting pots or ice-cream containers for planting seeds.
- Bean seeds.
- Separate buckets of sand, loam, and compost to adjust the soil mixture.
- Magnifying glasses.
- Newspaper on which to spread soil.
- Pictures of different landscapes—mountains, desert, seacoast, valley, pasture, etc.
- Cans or plastic cups with holes in the bottom and some stones to stop holes blocking up.
- Soils (sand, loam, clay).
- Simple weighing scales.
- Plastic measuring cups with a 100ml capacity.
- Dishes to collect water that drains through the soil.
- Sandboxes in which to make model mountains and valleys.
- Watering cans.
- Electric fans.
- Jars with water and a soil mixture.
- Raw materials for compost.
- Surgical gloves for mixing compost.
- Two fish tanks in which to put layers of soil, compost, etc.
- Black paper to keep the "wormeries" dark.

The children soon recognized how many of the things they use every day depend in turn on the land.

Russell raised the notion of different soils: if you wanted to plant some corn or some beans, would you plant them on the beach? in the desert? on a rocky shelf in the mountains? Vegetables don't grow on the beach. There can be "good soils" and "poor soils."

Making Your Own Soil

RUSSELL: How could we work out what is a good soil, and what is not?

TINA: We could make a race.
RUSSELL: How do you mean?
TINA: We could plant some plants that all start together and see which one wins.
RUSSELL: Why would some plants grow faster than others?
TINA: Some soils are not healthy.
RUSSELL: Do plants need other things to grow?
TINA: We'd have to give them water and light.

Russell suggested that beans might be suitable to grow. The children planned what they would do, discussing at some length what a fair race would entail—what size pots and where to put them, how much soil,

Unit Outline

GETTING STARTED: THIS COMES FROM THAT

MAKING YOUR OWN SOIL

SOIL IS A MIXTURE

DIFFERENT SOILS IN DIFFERENT PLACES

INVESTIGATING SOILS

HOW ARE SOILS MADE?

LIFE, DEATH AND DECAY

PROTECTING AND IMPROVING SOILS: WHAT HAVE WE LEARNED?

RUSSELL'S REFLECTIONS

SUGGESTED AUSTRALIAN SCIENCE PROFILE OUTCOMES
The unit spans levels 1, 2, and 3 in the strands:

- Earth and Beyond (Earth, sky and people; The changing earth)
- Working Scientifically (Planning investigations; Conducting investigations; Processing data; Evaluating findings; Using science; Acting responsibly)

matching the amounts of sunlight and water. Russell explained that the plants would take some weeks to appear. The children decided it was too risky planting only one bean per pot—that bean might die, or the seed might be "sick." They put four seeds in each pot.

Then there was the matter of choosing a "good" soil. The children went out in pairs, armed with trowels and ice-cream containers. Some went to damp places, others dry; some went to garden beds, others to far corners. Back in the classroom, they compared their soils, looking at color, moisture, and texture. Miles actually had two worms in his sample. The children speculated on which soils would grow beans best. They were surprised at the differences in the samples, all from within the school grounds.

Russell set out three additional buckets—one with sand, another with loam, a third with decomposing matter from the compost bin. He invited the children to modify their soil if they wanted. Some added sand. Nearly everyone added compost. They mixed their ingredients, set up the pots for planting, and labeled them.

Soil Is a Mixture

The children made a long list of things you might find in soil: worms, insects, dead birds, bugs, rubbish, creeping crawly things, water, pipes, underground rivers, plants, weeds, seeds, ants, ant holes, worm tunnels, animal manure, compost, roots, animals homes, growing carrots, rotting things, pebbles, potatoes, fallen apples, roots, germs, ladybugs, bones, spiders, bottles, buried bodies.

Perhaps prompted by the earlier activity on making soil, they were comfortable with the idea that soil was a mixture, but it wasn't clear whether they thought all the things they had listed were soil or were simply found in soil. Russell questioned them further:

RUSSELL: What if a dog buries some bones. Are they part of the soil?

CHILDREN: Yes.
PETER: They turn into soil.
RUSSELL: How?
PETER: They break off.
LAURA: They rot. They make like (*pause*) a mulch.
RUSSELL: What if I left a shovel in the ground? Say, for five hundred years.
JOSEPH: If you left it for a long long time, it would turn into soil.
JONATHON: It's just like the rubbish bins, you know they put it into a great big empty place and leave it. Glass and things stay there forever, but plastic and things will just (*pause*) disappear.
TINA: Plastic will just (*pause*) melt.

The children spread their soils on newspaper and looked more closely. They rubbed the soil, smelled it, broke up clods, and looked at bits of dirt through magnifying glasses. Russell had also set up a binocular microscope through which they could look at some sandy loam. They drew and wrote about what they found. Miles showed off the worms in his sample. Thea found a crawly thing in hers. That got everyone looking for living things, perhaps ones they could see with normal vision, perhaps ones they could only see through magnifying glasses. They were engrossed with the magnifying glasses and the microscope, looking at tiny pieces of rock, the shiny faces of sand grains, minute animals, and pieces of decayed plants.

The class talked about the things they had found in the soil, summarizing ideas into a group concept map (see Figure 1). They understood soil as a mixture, that the mixture can vary, and that it can change over time.

RUSSELL: Is clay soil?
CHILDREN: Yes.
RUSSELL: Is sand soil?
CHILDREN: Yes.

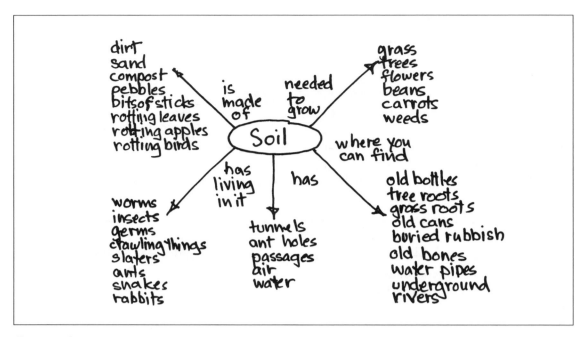

Figure 1: Group concept map

LAURA:	Sort of.
RUSSELL:	What do you mean, Laura? (*Laura doesn't answer*)
TINA:	It's not very good soil.
RUSSELL:	Does soil change?
CHILDREN:	Yes.
AMY:	It does change, because it gets in the tree roots, and when you take a tree and plant it somewhere else, you shift dirt.
PETER:	The wind can blow it around.
THEA:	People can shift soil around, in trucks.
MILES:	Tree roots move the soil as they grow.

Different Soils in Different Places

Just from looking around the school ground, the children were aware that different soils were found in different places. Some of the children lived in houses with back and front gardens. Russell asked them to have a look at the soils they had at home and compare them with the examples of sand, loam, and compost in the buckets at school.

· The children looked at magazine pictures of different places: a craggy mountain, a river valley, a desert, a rice field, a wheat field being ploughed, a lush cattle pasture. Russell asked the children how they thought the soils might be different in the different places. The children all agreed that the desert was dry and dusty, there wasn't much soil on the mountain crags, the rice fields were mud. They decided the river valley and the wheat field were probably the best soil, or perhaps the pasture: where plants grew well, they argued, the soil was good. Russell suggested that rainfall was a factor, but the children were focused on soils.

The checked their beans, to see if any were sprouting yet.

Investigating Soils

Visiting a nursery

Some children already knew that soils can be purchased and delivered to your garden. They went on a field trip to a local nursery, where a gardener showed them different soils: sandy loams, river sand, mountain soil, peat. The children collected samples of each kind of soil. The gardener explained that some plants prefer particular soils, and that people try to change their soil by mixing sand or mountain soil with it so they can grow particular plants. People also buy compost to dig into their gardens or spread on the top.

When he was arranging the visit, Russell had asked the gardener to talk about the "structure" of soils: whether it forms clods, and the number of tunnels and air passages within it. The gardener talked about the roles of sand, compost, worms, and microorganisms in improving the structure of soil for gardens.

On the walk back to school, Russell took the group past a small excavation so the children could see layers of soil near the top, and the rock below.

Soil's capacity to hold water

Back in class, the children discussed what the gardener had told them at the nursery and described things they had seen. The idea of soil structure seemed to be important to them. They liked the idea of worms and animals playing vital roles in improving soil structure. They also responded to the idea that different soils held water differently. Maybe that was why beach sand was nearly always dry—it wasn't simply the effect of the sun.

They set up experiments with sand, loam, mountain soil, and clay to compare water retention. They agreed on the following plan:

- Each group would put holes in the bottom of four cans and cover the bottom of each can with stones so the holes couldn't become blocked up.
- They would fill each cans about half full with one of the kinds of soil, pack the soil down, and then weigh it.
- They would pour 100 milliliters of water into each sample, after placing a dish underneath to collect the water as it came through.
- They would compare the water collected after five minutes, one hour, and three hours.

The results varied quite a bit, even between the same soils. The children listed possible reasons (spilled water, inaccurate measurements, soil packed down tighter in some cans than in others, different-size cans) and ways the experiment could be made fairer. Even so, the results showed convincingly that different soils have different capacities for holding water.

RUSSELL: So if you had very sandy soil, how could you make it hold water better?

TONY: You could put clay or mountain soil in it.

RUSSELL: And what if you had clay, which was always either too dry and hard or too wet?

TONY: You could put sandy soil with it.

How Are Soils Made?

The children, as a group, were aware that soils change over time, as a result of the decomposition of organic material, erosion, and the intervention of human beings. In this section they investigated erosion and sedimentation, volcanoes and the formation of mountains, and the decay of organic materials.

Erosion and sedimentation

Modeling in the sandbox

The children's basic activity was to build model mountains and valleys in the sandbox. Working with little direction, the children made models of mountains, rivers, cliffs, and lakes and investigated the effects of wind and water by pouring water on them with a watering can or hose, blowing on them with a fan, and leaving them in the weather for a few days. They talked about the effects of erosion in the sandbox, how the sand on the mountains tended to end up in the valley, shifted there by the wind or rivulets of water. They also tried different methods of preventing erosion—mixing straw in the sand, cloaking sand hills with grassy turf, covering them with cloth, building "terraces" to resist rivulets down the side, and keeping them moist by spraying them with water. At the end, they made posters on ways to reduce erosion.

Russell then played a short video showing dust storms and wind erosion on farm land and demonstrating how erosion can be prevented by planting crops.

Predict, then observe sedimentation

They mixed together different-sized grains of soil, sand, and pebbles in jars of water and left the jars to settle, observing the rate at which the different particles settled and also the layers that formed.

Finally, they went on another field trip to collect soil samples near a river, noticing that soil is laid down in layers and comparing the texture and composition of the different layers. Russell reminded them of the layer of soil that they had seen in the excavation. He showed them pictures in which the layers could be clearly seen.

Mountains, volcanoes, and rocks

When they were exploring erosion, Russell's students had raised the question of where the rock materials came from in the first place. The key point Russell wanted to make (and the children needed to understand) was that rocks don't come only from sedimentation: they are also pushed up from inside the earth as molten lava and in the gigantic upheavals that create mountains.

Russell explained that some rocks are formed over millions of years by sedimentation, and reminded them of the layers they had seen in the pictures of rocks. But he also discussed the "ultimate source"—magma from volcanoes and mountains pushed out from the interior of the earth. Russell showed pictures and talked about some recent volcanoes that had erupted in the Philippines and New Guinea and talked about the forming of Mt. Gambier in South Australia about 4,000 years ago. He showed the children some pieces of basalt and granite, formed from the cooling of volcanic lava. He resisted going further into the topic of volcanoes and the interior of the earth: he wanted to retain the focus on soils.

Life, Death, and Decay

Russell's class had shown in earlier discussions that they were aware that plants and animals and some human rubbish, in time, turn to soil. In this section Russell focused on the value of compost and the problems that nonbiodegradable materials pose.

RUSSELL: Does soil change?
ANA: The sun can change the soil. If it's a hot place, it can be so hot that the soil just melts into sand.
LAURA: The sun can make the soil dry.
JONATHON: It changes because worms move it. They eat it and take it to another place.

THINGS TO PUT IN	THINGS TO LEAVE OUT	NOT SURE
grass clippings	big pieces of metal	chop bones
leaves	plastic	newspaper
vegetable peels	bricks	small pieces of wood
table scraps	old clothes	old nails
manure	big pieces of wood	
soil		

Table 1: Things to put in a compost bin and things to leave out

Making compost

The children talked about the things they could put into a compost bin and things better left out (see Table 1). Russell drew their attention to the differences between this table and the ideas they had come up with earlier—for example, that bones, plastic, and metal would turn to soil. Some of the children simply weren't sure; others thought that these materials would eventually turn to soil, but not as fast as the "soft" materials they had listed as things to include.

Russell read from a garden guide about how to make compost: put layers of soil and other materials into a bin or box, and mix it all up every few days. The guide said the rate of decomposition depended on temperature and the amount of air (oxygen) available. If the material was in a bin or bucket, it would get warm as it decayed and stay warm; if it were mixed up every few days, air could get to it.

The children, with Russell's guidance, designed an experiment to examine the effects of mixing. They set up five buckets, each filled with the same layers. Russell sent a letter home, explaining what the children would do, and asking for help in providing vegetable matter for the compost. He made it clear that the children would wear surgical gloves when mixing the compost. The children brought table scraps and vegetable peels from home; Russell provided grass clippings, leaves, and soil from the school grounds.

They cut slits in two of the buckets so that air could enter through the sides as well as the top. They numbered and labeled their buckets as follows:

1. Slits, no hand mixing.
2. Slits, hand mixing every three days.
3. No slits, no hand mixing.
4. No slits, hand mixing every three days.
5. No slits, small pieces of hard rubbish (brick, timber, metal, plastic) mixed in with soil, hand mixing every three days.

The children had a great time, putting on their surgical gloves and stirring the compost.

Two weeks later, they discussed what they had found. Russell explained that tiny animals and bacteria were mainly responsible for decomposing the materials and turning them into soil.

Setting up a "wormery"

Some of the children knew how worms improve soil, by mixing it, by tunneling in it, and by dropping their excrement in it. They wanted to set up a "wormery." With Russell's help, they decided to set up two fish tanks with layers of sand, compost, and soil, and introduce worms to one of them. There was some planning to do: what would the worms need in order to live? how wet should the soil be? do worms prefer darkness or light?

The children suggested answers to these questions. To check their answers, they went on a worm hunt outside, and also talked to their families about the sorts of environments that worms like. They made a cardboard cover (from black construction paper) to go over each tank, to keep it dark except for special and brief viewing times. They decided to monitor the tanks daily to see that the worms were staying in the soil and that the soil was not too dry or too damp.

In the meantime, Russell provided books about worms and compost and even a story about a worm farm that produces worm excrement for sale.

Waiting time

Russell then went on to another unit for the next two weeks; the students simply turned the compost, observed the worms, and checked the beans.

Protecting and improving soils: what have we learned?

To complete the unit, the children compared the results of their experiments. Russell assigned them to three different groups

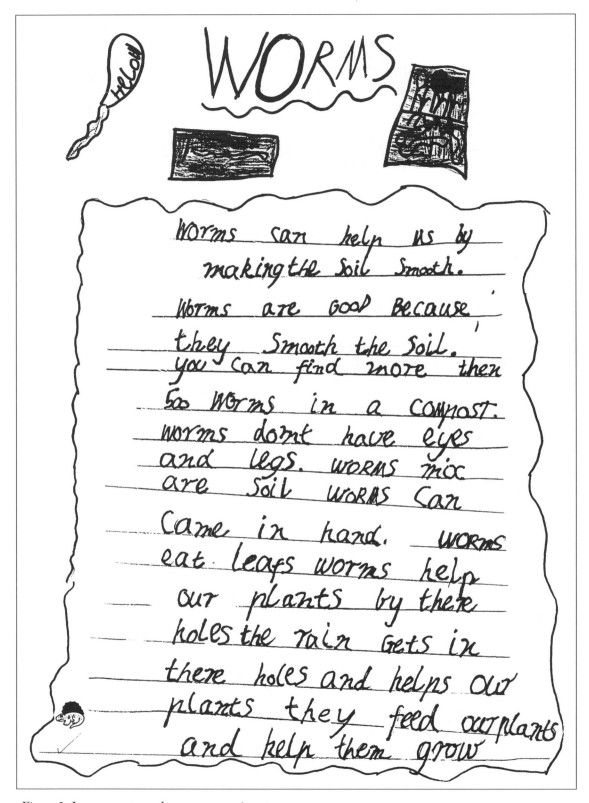

Figure 2: Jason reports on the worms experiment

in which to report on one or another of the beans experiment, the worms experiment, and the compost experiment, drawing pictures and writing to explain what they had found (see Figure 2).

Then they reviewed what they had done in the unit—why soil is important, what soil contains, how soils are made, and the idea that things turn to soil.

Russell then turned their attention to what humans can do (or avoid doing) to help conserve and improve soil. The children as a group came up with reducing erosion, making sure that plant and animal materials are cycled back into the soil, and managing household waste. And they knew how to make compost!

Russell's reflections

The open structure of the unit and the activities suited the children very well—the children could work on the activities in ways that suited their individual interests and knowledge. This was so whether modeling in the sandbox, mixing soils to grow beans, reading books on volcanoes, or looking after the worms. The unit responded to the children's interest in soils, but not so well to their fantasies and questions about worlds below the surface. Perhaps this was the time for imaginative adventures with the Hobbit and other such creatures; the disclosures of paleontology and theories of the core of the earth could come later.

The Story Within

Young children have fascinating and humorous ideas about what's inside their bodies:

Belly buttons help you breathe.
Many little brains help make up our brain.
Your heart is behind your tummy.
We have red blood on one side and blue blood on the other side.
We have two holes—one for food and one for air.
Food goes down to your legs.
Bigger people have more bones.
All bones look the same and are the same shape.
Bones are not joined together.

This unit helps children identify, describe, and discuss their bodies. They will consider both internal features such as heart, stomach, and skeleton and external features such as eyes, ears, and mouth. They will begin to understand the idea of a functional system—sets of components that work together with a particular purpose, such as the skeletal system, the respiratory system, and the arm-hand system.

Getting Started: What Do You Know About Your Body?

Ask children to reflect on what they know about their body and the functions of different parts and to draw a picture of their body and what they think is inside.

Materials

- Humanlike puppet.
- Large roll of chart paper and marker pens.
- Matchsticks or straight pins and cardboard cutouts of bones to make model skeletons.
- Some animal bones (from a butcher, for example) to inspect.
- X-ray pictures showing human bones.
- A water pump (a fish tank pump, for example).
- Balloons to simulate lungs.
- Stethoscope or cardboard tubes to use as listening tubes.
- Clear plastic bags, stockings, and a variety of foods (e.g., cooked oatmeal and pieces of soft foods) to simulate the stomach and intestines.

● ●

Unit Outline

GETTING STARTED: WHAT DO YOU KNOW ABOUT YOUR BODY?

PLANNING INVESTIGATIONS: FORMULATING QUESTIONS

INVESTIGATING: EXTERNAL AND INTERNAL SYSTEMS

SHARING AND ASSESSING FINDINGS

SUGGESTED AUSTRALIAN SCIENCE PROFILE OUTCOMES
The unit spans levels 1, 2, and 3 in the strands:

- Life and Living (Structure and function)
- Working Scientifically (Planning investigations; Conducting investigations; Using science; Acting responsibly)

It is also relevant to levels 1 and 2 in Life and Living (Biodiversity, change and continuity).

One approach might be to ask children to explain to a puppet what is in their bodies.

The puppet's opening question might be, What do you know about your body? or What are the main parts of your body?

Corrie's students first suggested external things like arms, legs, head, and so on. Corrie drew a large body outline on the board, putting in the various features as the children suggested them. For each part, the puppet asked What is this for? or What do you do with this? so thinking was oriented to function and systems.

The discussion can be extended to internal systems by having the puppet ask a question like What can you tell me about the inside of your body? Children have many different ideas about where organs are and what they do. Corrie had to be careful not to impose "right answers" at this stage: her purpose was to encourage children to share their current understanding.

Alternatively, Jodie drew an outline around several children and cut the figures out. Every child then drew an organ that she or he knew and stuck it on one of the figures where they thought it went inside the body. Because the outlines were full size, the children had to think about the full size of organs they drew.

Jodie asked them to label on one figure "all the things that can move." The children experimented with their own bodies. They identified things that bend, like joints and knuckles; things that turn, like necks and legs; things that flex, like muscles, lips, and nostrils; things that roll, like eyes and tongue. They also experimented with the movements that occur during breathing. Some children wanted to add that blood flows and hearts pump.

Jodie asked the children to show on their drawings what connected to what. What does the heart connect to? What about the lungs? Most children simply saw the organs as individual features. Many drew stylized images of organs like the heart and kidney. Few knew how the organs work together as teams to make the whole body function. Few knew where their stomachs are (often putting it in their lower abdomen) or what happens to food after it leaves their mouth. (Does it float around in blood in the legs?)

Drawing around each child's body and having them draw what is inside is time consuming—not to mention space consuming! Move to the corridor to allow the whole group to participate. If you can enlist parents to help for that day, it will be much easier to get around to each child, talk to them, and perhaps scribe their ideas onto a drawing.

Planning Investigations: Formulating Questions

Asking questions helps children develop, clarify, modify, and extend their ideas. Their questions can stimulate other children to think about aspects they might not otherwise consider. In addition, children's questions guide lesson planning, enabling closer links between teaching and children's interests and needs. Their questions generally fall into one of these categories:

- Questions to investigate (What would happen if. . . ? If this, then what. . . ? I wonder whether. . . ?)
- Procedural questions (How can we find out. . . ? What should we do to. . . ?)
- Sense questions (How does this relate to. . . ? Where else have we seen something like this? Does this mean. . . ?)

Formulating questions, especially good questions, is a skill that children need help to develop. First help them know what a question is, then help them recognize and formulate good questions.

Knowing a question

Though children may ask many questions at home, a questioning environment has to be created in school. Help children recognize what a question is by:

- Acknowledging examples. (That's an interesting question you just asked.)
- Setting up question-and-answer times. (Would anyone like to ask Natalie a question about her news?)
- Modeling. (I have a question that I would like to ask Natalie. My question is . . .)
- Encouraging and supporting questioning, from children to teacher, teacher to children, child to child.

Frequently, children make statements rather than ask questions. You can rephrase the statement as a question or ask the child to think about the statement in a different context:

CHILD: The sky is blue.
TEACHER: Is it always blue?
CHILD: No.
TEACHER: Perhaps your question could be, When is the sky blue?

Young children also often ask questions they already know the answer to or questions that are too complex to answer satisfactorily. Help them focus on part of the question only, or turn the question into another one that is more fruitful. For example, Why is the sky blue? could be modified to When is the sky blue?

Identifying good questions

Help children evaluate and revise their questions into ones that are interesting, useful, and researchable. This can be achieved by

- Brainstorming a list of questions.
- Deciding which are the good questions.
- Discussing why each question is good.
- Rewriting questions to make them better.

A question is interesting if there is some contention about the answer. A question is useful if the answer is seen as worth having. A question is researchable if its wording suggests ways that it can be answered and the sort of information that is needed.

When turning a child's question like Why is the sky blue? into a researchable one like When is the sky blue? there is always the risk that an interesting question will become an uninteresting one, but the reverse can also be the case.

Skills in asking good questions and using them as springboards to learning and further questions take many years to develop. They are part of "working scientifically": planning and conducting investigations, making sense of information, evaluating findings, using science, and acting responsibly.

Jodie's children asked many questions, including:

How come only your bottom jaw moves?
How does your leg move?
Why do you need to breathe?
Does your heart go faster if you want to move your finger?
How do your intestines move and go around helping your body to work?

Why do you need veins?
Why do you have blood in your body?
Do children have as much blood as adults?

Jodie took account of these questions in her planning, though not all of them were answered. She introduced questions of her own as well, like What parts of your body work together in breathing? and How are our bodies similar? different?

Investigating: External and Internal Systems

The investigations below are the basis for helping children extend their knowledge and understanding. Generally, the activities address the following questions: (for external—sensory, motor)

- What does it do?
- How are we the same and different?
- How does this knowledge help us?

(for internal systems—skeletal, circulatory, respiratory, digestive)

- What's inside?
- What does it do?
- Can we make a model?
- How does this knowledge help us?

In each case, the central ideas are function, systems, and models or representations. Children reflect on similarities and differences in their bodies, and on how we use our knowledge of our bodies to stay healthy and act responsibly.

The discussions during and after each activity are important. Children see more clearly the purpose of their investigations and the progression of their understanding. They are helped to develop a systems view of the body as they listen to one another's interpretations.

External features:

Do we all have. . . ?
Have children list external features that they all have—arms, eyes, mouth—perhaps noting that males and females have different genitalia. Ask them to compare human features with features of other animals (primates, cats and dogs, birds).

What is it for?
Ask children to consider the function of particular systems:

- How both eyes move together, how eyes respond to sudden changes in light.
- How arms and hands work to pick up an object and put it somewhere (perhaps one child can give instructions to another who is blindfolded).
- How they shift their balance as they walk or when they pick up a piece of paper from the floor.

From these activities, children begin building concepts of the function of different body parts and of systems that work together.

Are all hands the same?
Have children compare similarities and differences in their body parts—the shapes of hands and feet and bodies generally; skin color, eyes, tongue curling, footprints. Children should see the diversity of physical features and discuss some of the factors that influence them, like ethnicity, heredity, health, diet, injury.

How does this knowledge help us?
Ask children to reflect on who is helped by knowing how our bodies work—doctors; physiotherapists; sports coaches; safety officials in industry; designers of furniture, cars, and equipment.

Skeletal system

Children's ideas
Have children use matchsticks to create models of their skeleton, thinking about how many bones they have and which bones connect to which. (They could sing a song like Dem Bones.)

Bones in different animals

Ask children to compare the shape and size of some human bones to bones of other animals. Which bone could it be? Let children examine animal bones under a microscope or magnifying glass and draw what they see.

Working with a model skeleton: structure and function

Have children examine a model skeleton to see how all of the bones are joined together, then let them refer to charts or books to see how the muscles help them move.

Point out the important positioning of some bones for protection of vital organs—ribs/heart, skull/brain.

Ask the students to demonstrate what it would be like to move if we didn't have any joints.

Bring in copies of X-rays so that students can see human bones and perhaps how they can break.

How does this knowledge help us?

Have children talk about ways bones are broken and repaired and how they can protect themselves. Ask them to identify how we use science and how we use it to act responsibly.

Circulatory system

What do the heart and blood do?

Ask the children to run very fast in place and then, in pairs, let them listen to each other's heart using a toilet tissue roll or even a stethoscope. They will discover that the rate of the heartbeat changes with exercise. By helping them feel their pulse (in the neck or the wrist), you can establish the link between heartbeat and the blood pulsing through the veins.

How do they work?

Let children extract information from books and charts to explain in their own words how blood is pumped around the body. Be sure that they relate the heart to veins and arteries and recognize that blood brings oxygen and "foods" to all parts of the body and collects wastes.

Make a model

Ask children to think about the heart as a pump. Set up a working model of a water pump (one from a fish tank, for example) to demonstrate how the water is continuously circulated. Possibly demonstrate what happens if a lot of water (blood) is lost. You could help the children make up a song like the following (to the tune of *The Farmer in the Dell*):

> The heart is like a pump,
> The heart is like a pump,
> Pumping blood to help you grow,
> The heart is like a pump!

How does this knowledge help us?

Lead a discussion about exercise, rest, and relaxation—the heart needs all of these to stay healthy.

The respiratory system

What do lungs do?

Let children investigate their own breathing—the rise and fall of their lungs and, alternately, the movement of their diaphragm and stomach. Ask them to try breathing through their mouth and then through their nose, perhaps blocking off one, then both, nostrils. Prompt them to think about the "pipes" that might link nose, mouth, and lungs and how they can choose nose breathing or mouth breathing.

Can we make a model?

Have children make model lungs by blow-ing up balloons and letting them deflate. Discuss how this is like the movement and function of the lungs and mouth. (There is an important difference: with a balloon they blow air in that makes the balloon expand, but in breathing they expand their lungs using muscles, then the air rushes in to fill the space; to deflate the balloon, they simply release the end and the air rushes out, but in breathing, they use muscles to squeeze their lungs and push the air out.)

How does this knowledge help us?

Have the children watch films and/or read about respiratory illnesses such as asthma or emphysema. They could also investigate a special breathing apparatus, like scuba gear.

The digestive system

Children's ideas

Canvas students' ideas about what happens to food when they eat it.

What happens to food?

Have children refer to books and charts to find out about the passage of food from the mouth to the stomach through the small and large intestine and into the rectum. Explain that the body takes what it needs from the small intestine and leaves the rest to be eliminated.

Help the children understand that when they go to the toilet they are eliminating leftover food.

Let students, in pairs, listen to each other's stomach sounds using a toilet tissue roll or a stethoscope.

Can we make a model?

Simulate the stomach using a plastic bag and some food such as a banana, biscuits, and orange juice. Squeeze the food until it no longer resembles the individual food items but is liquefied and ready to move onto the small intestine. While doing this you could ask the children to pretend to eat the food items and discuss how the food gets from their mouths into the stomachs. They should talk about such bodily parts as the teeth, tongue, throat, and esophagus.

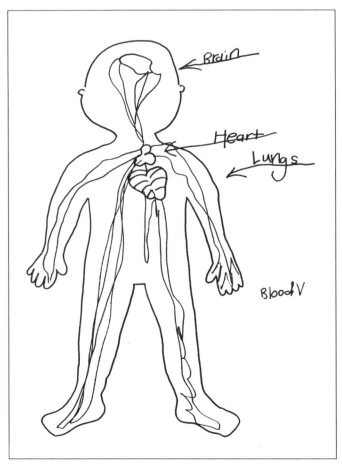

Figure 1: Emma's body

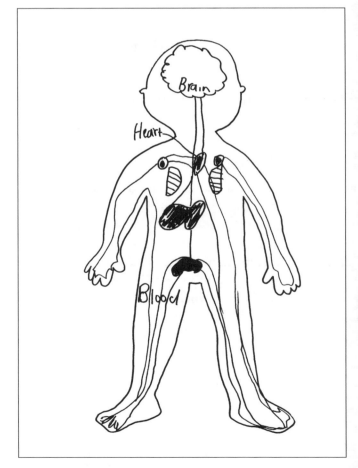

Figure 2: Bill's body

Simulate the small intestine by pushing either the squashed food from above or cooked oatmeal through a stocking. Show how the small intestine curls around in the body and compare this simulation to a 3-D model or a drawing.

How does this knowledge help us?

Talk about how we need to eat the right foods and maintain a balanced diet so that our body can get what it needs. Discuss hygiene as well as diet.

Sharing and Assessing Children's Findings

Ask the children, this time individually, once again to draw and describe what they think is inside them and what it does (see Figures 1 and 2). Let them compare their ideas now with those at the start of the unit to indicate progress and unresolved difficulties. As well as the placement, size, and function of organs, watch for connections that the children make between organs.

Reflect on how the scientific knowledge of our bodies is used—not only in medicine, but in design, sports, theatre, marketing, workplace safety. Let the children suggest more responsible things they might do in caring for their own bodies.

Jodie found that her children

- Were better able to view the body as a whole and were beginning to understand that what happens to one part effects other parts.
- Were more aware of the role blood played and saw it as a link between the organs.

Our Place in Space

The Teacher's Story: What We Did

I saw the unit as helping the children develop their understanding of outer space and our place in space. Much of it was fact finding—about the planets, nebulae and stars, the sun and moon, space travel and its history, living in space, aliens from other planets.

Within this broad structure, I wanted the children to be able to follow their own interests and work at their own levels. Accordingly they did much of their learning through projects, videos, and reading. We also went on a field trip.

To help them focus their learning, I asked them to produce things: contribute to two class "big books" on space, write reports and letters, draw, paint, write stories and poems, make rockets. Through this we were also able to integrate language, art, math, and technology into the unit.

I worked with the children, helping them find information and understand it and observing as they planned, evaluated, and reported on their projects.

Prior views

To find out what children knew about space, we discussed their views of everything they understood about outer space. I recorded their ideas on a flipchart, and we made a group concept map.

Questions

We then talked about what it was that we would like to know more about. We came up with a list of questions that became the basis of our class investigations.

Videos, books, field trips

We used videos and books to try to find some of the answers to the questions we had, and visited a local space observatory. The field trip was an excellent opportunity to investigate some of the facts the children had found but had difficulty imagining.

Fascinating facts

As the children researched, they found a number of very interesting pieces of information. Those things that were particularly

Materials

- Books and videos about outer space, space travel, and living in space.

```
• • • • • • • • • • • • • • • • • • • • • • • • • •
```

Unit Outline

THE TEACHER'S STORY: WHAT WE DID

- Prior views
- Questions
- Videos, books, field trips
- Fascinating facts

INTEGRATING OTHER CURRICULUM AREAS

COMPLETING THE UNIT: LOOKING BACK

SUGGESTED AUSTRALIAN SCIENCE PROFILE OUTCOMES
The unit spans levels 3 and 4 in the strands:

- Earth and Beyond (Our place in space)
- Working Scientifically (Planning investigations; Conducting investigations)

interesting or hard to imagine were recorded as "Fascinating Facts." I added ideas to the list from time to time—the sizes of the planets, for example. It showed them that I was learning too and enabled me to guide their thinking from time to time. For example, we explored the size of planets further in math by making scale models of the solar system.

Integrating Other Curriculum Areas

Asking students to analyze and report on information in different ways enabled me to integrate curriculum areas:

- We made a math "big book" on space.
- We wrote fiction about aliens and letters home from space.
- We designed space rockets.
- We examined space food and discussed how we could live in space.

Completing the Unit: Looking Back

To complete the unit, everyone wrote individually about all the things we had done as a class and what we had learned.

Figure 1 is nine-year-old Amy's summary of what the class did. Looking at a unit from a child's perspective can sometimes give greater insight about

- How children come to understand.
- How children interpret class projects and lessons.
- What children have understood about the topic being investigated by the class.
- How children relate class work to their own personal life.
- What children like doing.

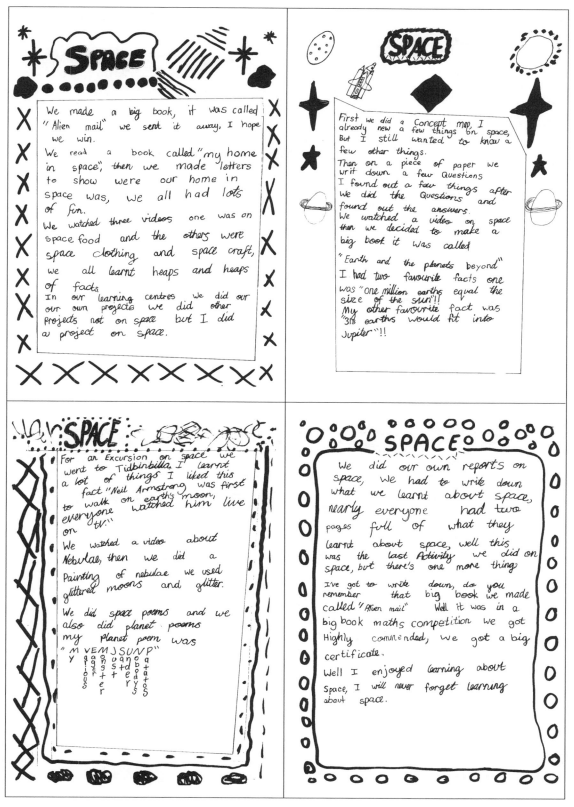

We made a big book, it was called "Alien mail" we sent it away, I hope we win.
We read a book called "my home in space", then we made letters to show were our home in space was, we all had lots of fun.
We watched three videos one was on space food and the others were space clothing and space craft, we all learnt heaps and heaps of facts.
In our learning centres we did our own projects we did other projects not on space but I did a project on space.

First we did a Concept map, I already new a few things on space, But I still wanted to know a few other things.
Then on a piece of paper we writ down a few Questions I found out a few things after we did the Questions and found out the answers.
We watched a video on space then we decided to make a big book it was called
"Earth and the planets beyond"
I had two favourite facts one was "one million earths equal the size of the sun"!!
My other favourite fact was "318 earths would fit into Jupiter"!!

For an Excursion on space we went to Tidbinbilla, I learnt a lot of things I liked this fact "Neil Armstrong was first to walk on earth's moon, everyone watched him live on tv."
We watched a video about Nebulae, then we did a Painting of nebulae we used glittered moons and glitter.
We did space poems and we also did planet poems my Planet poem was
"M V E M J S U N P"
Y a a a u a e e a
  g n r p n p r t
  i i c i t d b a
  o u u t u ... y t
  u s r e r r   o
  s   r ... s   s

We did our own reports on space, We had to write down what we learnt about space, nearly everyone had two pages full of what they learnt about space, well this was the last Activity we did on space, but there's one more thing
I've got to write down, do you remember that big book we made called "Alien mail" Well it was in a big book maths competition we got Highly commended, we got a big certificate.
Well I enjoyed learning about Space, I will never forget learning about space.

Figure 1

They Don't Tell the Truth About the Wind

Planning the Unit

This unit is presented as an account of how three teachers working together developed their ideas and planned and presented the unit.

Why weather?

Many topics provide a suitable context for a unit focused on working scientifically. We chose weather because the topic is directly relevant to the children and their communities; presents rich opportunities for investigating, using science, and acting responsibly; and fits easily with the idea of learning science in a social context, where concepts, processes, and human purposes are considered together. In addition, the concepts involved complement other units in this collection.

First thoughts

We began by writing down our own knowledge about working scientifically. At this point, we had not consulted any references: we were simply clarifying our ideas and what we thought would be important for the children.

We put our ideas into a rough concept map, discussing links and thinking about whether the map was complete.

Next we examined the science statement and the science profile, especially levels 1 and 2 in the profile, in light of our concept map. In practice the five organizers in the Working Scientifically strand interact

---

Materials

- Pre-made kites or materials to make kites (large plastic garbage bags for the kite and the tail, balsa wood for the frame, tape, long lengths of string, cardboard tubing on which to wind-up the string, a knife to cut the balsa wood).
- Balloons, big garbage bags, and plastic drink bottles.
- A long rod (e.g., a dowel or a yardstick) and string to make a beam-balance.
- A heat lamp, a piece of paper rolled into a tube (as a chimney), and a paper spiral (above the chimney).
- Plastic shopping bags or freezer bags and string to make parachutes.
- Clay objects for the parachutes to carry.
- Paper and scissors.
- Pins and drinking straws (or nails and popsicle sticks) to make windmills.

Unit Outline

This unit, through a study of weather, draws together ideas about working scientifically that are woven through the preceding units and detailed in *A Statement on Science for Australian Schools and Science—A Curriculum Profile for Australian Schools.*

AUSTRALIAN SCIENCE PROFILE SUGGESTED OUTCOMES
The unit spans levels 1 and 2 in the strands:

- Working Scientifically (Planning investigations; Conducting investigations; Using science; Acting responsibly)
- Earth and Beyond (Earth, sky, and people)

and overlap. "Using science" and "Acting responsibly" were new components for us and not very apparent in our map, so we added them to produce the map in Figure 1.

What does it mean, to work scientifically?
According to the statement and profile, working scientifically is not only about developing skills, but also about understanding

what science is, being able to choose to work scientifically as opposed to unscientifically. In other words, the children need to reflect on characteristics of science. There are many clues in the profile and statement. For example, page 4 of the profile lists unifying ideas:

- To understand something or to solve a problem, it is helpful to analyze its parts.
- Change occurs by interaction.
- Interaction and change are caused by transfer of energy and/or matter.
- Science is conducted partly to create meaning in our world and partly to improve the world.
- Working scientifically is an effective way of generating understanding and solving problems.

We considered also actual outcomes in the profile, relating them to the skills and to the nature of science. We developed a list of characteristics that became organizing ideas in our unit. They are highlighted in boxes in the theme descriptions.

Guiding questions
To help children with concept development, we are used to asking questions:

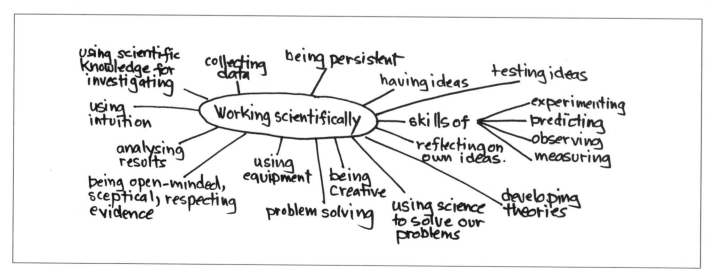

Figure 1: Concept map: Working scientifically

What do you see?

What do you mean by. . . ?

How do you explain. . . ?

What would happen if. . . ?

How are these things the same?

We thought it would be helpful to have a parallel list of questions to guide working scientifically. Ours is shown in Figure 2.

Thinking About Weather

We began by sharing our existing knowledge. We spent some time looking in books and watching television weather reports. Statements that we found useful included:

Our earth is wrapped in a blanket of air called the atmosphere.

The sun is the engine which drives all our weather.

Air on the move is called wind.

Weather forecasters study how the air is moving.

Joy Richardson. *The Weather.*
London: Franklin Watts, 1992.

Earth's weather is an aspect of the natural world which we cannot control and can barely predict. Weather dictates where we live and what we wear, what crops we grow and how fruitful they will be. It takes lives with its immense uncontrollable power and gives life in the form of fresh water from rain and snow. The earth's complex weather system results from the energy from the sun and its effect on the waters of our

PLANNING INVESTIGATIONS
What do we already know about this? What is interesting about this? What do you think is happening? What do we need to find out? What is the question we want to answer? What could we do? What equipment would we need? Is that a good way? Is it fair? What's another way we could do it? Would that be better? Do some things have to be done in particular order? Where could we find out what we want to know? Who could help?

CONDUCTING INVESTIGATIONS
What do we need to do first? next? Who will do what? How do I use [this object]? Did we do it carefully? What do you think is going to happen? What should we write down? Does this suggest something else we need to look at?

PROCESSING DATA
What did we see? What does it mean? How could we show our results to others? How can we explain this? Does this result surprise us?

EVALUATING FINDINGS
Can we be sure about what we've got? Should we do it again? Should we try it another way? Have I seen something like this before? Does this make sense to me?

USING SCIENCE
Do other people use this knowledge? What for? Do people work scientifically as part of their daily life? Do we?
In what ways does this [knowledge or skill] help us?

ACTING RESPONSIBLY
Are we being thoughtful about safety? other people? animals and plants? the environment? How might [this knowledge or skill] be used to help others? to endanger others? conserve resources? How do people in the community use [this knowledge or skill]?

Figure 2: **Questions to help students work scientifically**

planet. (*1993 Science Calendar.* Boston: Museum of Science, 1992)

The science statement and the Earth and Beyond strand in the science profile gave us further suggestions:

- Identify ways that weather influences daily life, distinguish features of the weather, and relate them to patterns of behavior (level 1).
- Identify ways that we monitor and use information about the weather, describe changes in the weather (level 2), and investigate features of the weather as they relate to everyday behavior patterns.
- Illustrate ways in which weather changes the physical environment, relate changes in the weather to physical processes (level 3), and illustrate weather patterns caused by the relationship of the sun, earth, and moon.

With these outcomes in mind, we browsed through curriculum resources, looking for activities and ideas. We had no problems finding ideas for months of work!

Choosing weather topics

We had to constrain the unit and organize the ideas into a simple flow. We tried splitting weather into wind, rain, clouds, and temperature. On a blackboard we listed ideas and activities, starting with wind. The list became rather long, so we decided to use wind as the major emphasis and add ideas as appropriate on rain, clouds, and temperature.

Putting together a plan

Using questions about weather and the organizer headings from the profile's "Working Scientifically" strand, we developed a grid showing possible activities (see Tables 1-A and 1-B). We kept adjusting and revising until we had all the squares covered adequately, and felt that the activities would be interesting and useful.

Choosing a starting point and story line

The unit needed a theme, or story line, to tie it all together. We wanted to establish the theme in the opening activity, so that the children could see where the unit was headed from the start. After some discussion, we decided to use two simultaneous themes (see Table 2):

- Theme 1, Weather watch: Why is weather important? How can we understand the forecast? How are forecasts made? This theme began with children viewing a television weather report and ended with a visit from the TV weather forecaster. In between, children collected their own weather data and reflected on the importance of the weather for different people in the community.
- Theme 2, Air and Wind: What is the wind? What is air? How fast is the wind? We started by flying kites and feeling the wind. What can it do to other things, like parachutes and windmills? The windmills led us to measuring wind speed.

As well as engaging children's interest and setting the direction for the unit, watching a TV weather report and flying kites gave us opportunities to see what sort of experiences children had with concepts of wind and weather and what they understood by the term *air*.

Teaching the Unit

Theme 1: Weather watch

The TV weather report: science can help
▶ *Science is utilized in a human context and can help us in our daily lives.*

The children watched a video replay of the previous night's weather report. Many had seen this report or similar ones and were well aware that the community considers weather reports to be useful.

PLANNING INVESTIGATIONS What are our focus questions?	CONDUCTING INVESTIGATIONS How can we find out?	PROCESSING DATA What happened?
What is wind?	Carry out some simple experiments like popping balloons, displacing water with air, compressing air, and feeling hot air coming from a forced-air heater.	Discuss and list the qualities of air: has pressure, can be compressed, registers temperature, takes up space, moves.
How can we tell when there is wind?	Make some twirly items: a spinning arrow, wind chimes, kites. Hang ribbons outdoors. Dance with scarves on a windy day.	Each child could draw two pictures of the item they made, one when there is wind, one when it is still. What are the differences? Does the item need wind?
How can we measure how strong the wind is?	Use a wind sock or flags or a coat hanger and paper as a measuring device.	Create a class graph showing the changes in the measuring items with weak winds and strong winds.
What do wind directions mean?	Make a weather vane for the playground and observe over time the different directions and type of weather associated with each direction.	Make a chart showing possible wind directions and the expected weather.
Are there different types of wind?	Play blowing games to simulate different winds. Give names to different winds.	Report on different types of wind, giving them names and symbols.
What effect can the wind have?	Use a fan to simulate erosion in a sandbox and on the lawn. Why does grass stop erosion?	Explain what happened in the sandbox and on the lawn, how the wind causes erosion and how the lawn stops it.

Table 1-A. Planning grid for They Don't Tell the Truth About the Wind

The language of weather

▸ *In working scientifically, we use words from everyday life and also use some special "science words."*

After the replay, Sally asked the children to list words they remembered that the reporter had used. The children as a group were able to recall a remarkable number of words, given that the report is delivered so quickly. (Try it yourself!) They listed *moist, winds, stormy, forecast, showers, rain, cloud, cold front, sunny, high pressure, cloudy, low pressure, gusty, moving, satellite, frost.*

Many words in their list were technical,

EVALUATING FINDINGS What does this mean?	USING SCIENCE How could this help us?	ACTING RESPONSIBLY How can I help?
Discuss interpretations: that wind is air moving; things that make air move; why air rushes out of a balloon; high and low pressure.	Find some things at home that need wind, make wind or move in the wind—clothes drying, trees, fans, musical instruments, balloons, kites, sail boards.	What could we do on a really windy day to protect ourselves? animals? What might happen to trees and other plants? buildings?
What ways did we use to find out when there is wind? Which methods were the best? Why? What were the difficulties?	Which people in the community need to know if it is going to be windy? Create a collage.	Children create a story that explains how knowing about the wind helps to keep them safe.
Discuss the positioning of their measuring items. Could the wind get to them evenly? Were some placed in an area without wind? Could they move without wind?	Who are the people in our community who measure the wind? What methods do they use? How do they report to the community?	Has the wind ever damaged anything at your house or farm or in your garden? Find out about places that have been damaged by winds and hurricanes.
Would your findings about wind direction and weather always be true? Would they be the same in other places? How could we find out?	What are some things we do where the direction of the wind is important (sailing, flying, riding a bike, playing tennis)?	What are some ways we can protect ourselves (and animals, plants, and buildings) from winds or from winds in certain directions?
Relate erosion in the sandbox to erosion in the community; look for examples of ways it is prevented.	How do we protect gardens, farms, beaches, and forests from erosion? How do we protect our houses (inside and outside) from winds?	Plant some trees or grass at school. Grow some flowers in a place sheltered from the wind. Discuss their placement.

Table 1-B. Planning grid for They Don't Tell the Truth About the Wind

beyond 'ordinary' language. Understanding and using such words is part of working scientifically. We had to balance attention to the words of science with other aspects of working scientifically. We decided to use scientific language only when it was necessary and helpful. For that we needed a sense of which words the children were happy with already and the sorts of meanings they used. They made a list of words they associated with weather: *fog, wet, hot, cloudy, frost, cold, hail, snow, sunny, waves, windy, surfing, moist, seasons, stormy, gardening.*

How good was the forecast?
▸ *Through using a scientific approach we become better able to make predictions about events in the future. This can be a valuable aspect of science in daily life.*

The weather report had predicted that

THEME 1: WEATHER WATCH	THEME 2: AIR AND WIND
The TV weather report	Kites in the wind
What do we already know? The language of weather.	What do we already know? What makes the wind?
How good was the forecast?	Does air really exist? (Activities with air)
The weather watch	
Cloud cover	
Cloud shapes	What have we learned about air?
	Where does the wind come from? (Activities with 'little winds' and 'big winds')
What are we finding?	What do scientists do?
The weather watch continues.	Using the wind. (Making parachutes and windmills.)
A visit from an expert: We do what you do.	Measuring wind speed. Measuring wind direction.
What have we learned? Putting it all together.	What have we learned? Putting it all together.

Table 2. **Two themes**

the next day would be windy, "a good kite flying day." The prediction had come true. One student wondered aloud how "they" know in advance what the weather will be like—how they "made up" the forecast. An important aspect of science had surfaced: science often involves prediction of the course of natural events.

The weather watch

The children, in whole group discussion, considered which daily observations they might make and how they would record their findings. They decided to make four simple observations—sunshine, cloud, rain, and wind—and show their observations in pictures, one for each day. They talked about the drawings they might use—it was important that everyone understood the drawings.

Observations continued over four weeks, with children taking turns drawing a picture for each day (see Figure 3). (Saturday and Sunday were recorded on Monday.)

Cloud cover

▸ *Recording and looking for patterns in repeated observations is a common aspect of working scientifically.*

Because we wanted part of the observation to be quantitative, the children kept another chart on how much cloud was in the sky. They worked together to plan how they could estimate and record the cloud cover. For each weekday, they decided to make a square divided into quarters; they would then color sections of the square to show the proportion of the sky that was cloudy.

Cloud shapes

▸ *People who are effective in working scientifically use their imagination in making sense of their work and their world. Using metaphors is a common mode of understanding in science. Science can increase our sensitivity to the wonders of our universe and life on earth.*

The students' observation of clouds

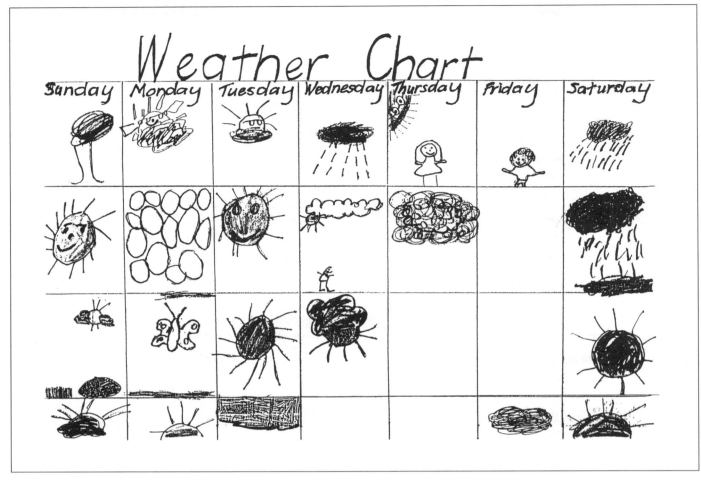

Figure 3: **An extract from the children's weather chart**

included a session where they looked at movement and shapes. ("What shapes can you see in the clouds?") The children recorded what they saw by making models using cotton wool on a blue painted background. Tegan captioned her model, "I saw a dragon puffing fire and smoke." This was the usual type of record. Some children commented instead on what they did: for example, Dana noted, "I use my amagnshen [imagination] and the clouds just look like a H," and Amanda wrote, "I saw a dinosaur in the air and I thought it was alive. But it was a cloud."

What are we finding?

▸ *Scientists often use predictions to test ideas about what might be happening (hypotheses). Their hypotheses and expectations then direct their observations.*

Midway through the weather watch, the children paused to review the data they had collected and to look for patterns in it. They focused on rain. From looking around them, how could they tell if it might rain soon? They decided fairly quickly that clouds were the important requirement and offered various predictors. From their suggestions, Sally helped the students form three researchable questions:

* Does it ever rain when there are no clouds at all?
* Are there ever clouds but no rain?
* Are some clouds more likely to mean rain than others?

The weather watch continues

To answer these three questions, the children first looked back over the big weather chart and their cloud cover charts. Then they each wrote down what they thought were the answers. They set these answers aside to look at again later. Then, for the next two weeks, their observations became more clearly focused—armed with theories they wanted to test, they looked carefully for signs. For example, they watched for rain and cloud cover throughout the day, not just at the time of completing the weather watch chart.

A visit from an expert—we do what you do

▶ *Working scientifically involves consulting experts—through talking to them or through their writings—and using their knowledge and skills.*

In the third week of the program, we were able to arrange for Katherine, the weather forecaster from a local television station, to come to visit the class.

The children explained their daily weather and cloud charts, their experiments with air (see theme 2), and their models of clouds. They had prepared questions in advance that they read from cards. Some of their questions focused on Katherine's role and her feelings about being on television. Others related more directly to science and her knowledge of the weather. One asked candidly, "How much do you know about the weather?" Katherine responded that she depended on scientists at the weather office for reports and forecasts, but she also showed the children that she understood the science involved.

Film of the visit and the children's scientific work was shown on television that night as part of the weather report. It effectively linked the children's activities to those of meteorologists and the wider community. The children understood this connection and enjoyed it: the community was making use of their science.

What have we learned?

Some days later, the children returned to the questions they had raised earlier, about clouds and rain. Now they were better able to draw generalizations from their weather

records: that rain needed to have clouds, but clouds didn't necessarily mean rain. They talked as well about the people involved in putting together and using weather reports: that there are weather stations around the country, where people take measurements and phone the information through to computers that plot graphs and maps; that scientists write reports for television, newspapers, and radio; that people who need to know the weather can get this information. They saw people using science.

Theme 2: Air and wind

This theme ran parallel with the weather-watch theme. It began with the children's flying kites and then moved to investigations of air and wind.

Kites in the wind

We already had a set of simple kites in the classroom: plastic cylinders like wind socks. There were enough for every child to have one. Outside in a strong wind, the children enjoyed investigating ways of getting the kites to fly and observing the motions.

What makes the wind?

Back inside, they talked about the experience: what it felt like as the kite went up; different techniques; why they ran into the wind, not with it.

The children were confident that the wind pushes against things, but what is the wind? Some said it was simply wind; others thought it was moving air. They weren't clear about what air is, either. Some said it was oxygen. Everyone knew it was all around us and that we need it to breathe. Was it substance?

Does air really exist?

▶ *Science often deals with aspects of our lives that are not readily apparent.*

To understand wind, children need some basic understanding of air. Air is a substance. Yet children can't see it or feel its weight in their hands. We wanted them to become convinced by their own observations that air exists, rather than accept it on the teacher's authority—simply to take it on authority would have been quite unscientific.

The children did the following investigations:

- *Blowing up a balloon or bag.* Rahul noted in his report, "We knew there was air in the bag because they blew up."
- *Deflating a balloon.* Children could feel the wind rushing out the end of the balloon and blowing against their skin.
- *Breathing in and out into a balloon.* Children felt the rise and fall of their chests or stomachs as they blew up the balloons and the air flow to and from their mouths.
- *Sitting on a balloon.* The air in the balloon makes a cushion.
- *Making garbage-bag balloons.* Children blew up plastic garbage bags of various sizes and sat on them.
- *Standing on balloons.* Children turned a table upside down and placed it on top of ten balloons. Then ten children stood on the table.
- *Weighing air.* Children balanced two inflated balloons on a hanging rod, then burst one, creating an imbalance.
- *Making air bubbles.* Children submerged plastic drink bottles (without lids) in water and squeezed them.

What have we learned about air?

▶ *Reporting observations clearly and linking different observations are crucial parts of working scientifically.*

The children performed these activities in different ways and in different orders, talking with each other about what they were doing and what they were finding. Only at the end did Sally try to draw it all together. This strategy encouraged the children to make their own links between the activities and to relate what they were doing to their observations of the wind and kites and even car tires.

Children were developing the skills of reporting evidence, linking ideas, using information, and interpreting what occurred.

Where does the wind come from?

▶ *Investigation in science builds on scientific knowledge that we have developed previously.*
▶ *Attempting to answer questions we have about our environment is a fundamental aspect of working in a scientific way.*

Deciding that the wind is moving air did not resolve for the children where the wind came from or how it was formed. We hoped the previous series of experiments would help the children better understand wind and investigate its properties. Some children thought the wind came from God (or particular gods—The North Wind, The South Wind). Some thought it came from clouds. Some felt it came from itself—it was like an animal that could decide to "wake up and rush around."

A common element in all the children's explanations was that the wind makes the air move (just as it makes trees or a kite move). This is quite different from the idea that moving air is the wind. We sensed it would be difficult for children to make the transition from one idea to the other.

The first thing we tried was to shift attention to "little" winds—breathing, deflating balloons, heating air in the room to produce vertical currents. If children could identify the causes of these little winds, we felt, they might begin to understand that when something makes air move, it has produced a wind. This moving air, in turn, can make other things move.

Little winds and big winds

▶ *Developing and testing models of phenomena is a significant and frequent aspect of a scientific approach.*

Sally asked the children what they thought caused little winds, like breathing and a deflating balloon. The children had no trouble with this: when they breathed out, they caused the wind, and the wind consisted of moving air. The wind did not cause itself. When they deflated a balloon, the "tight" balloon caused the wind, and again the wind consisted of rushing air. In both cases, could the wind make things move? Yes—they could blow dust or pieces of paper or a propeller and make them move. The moving air crashed into the paper, like water from a hose.

Sally led the children toward a more difficult situation. She heated air to create an updraft that turned a paper spiral. She presented the activity as a demonstration, showing the children skills in observation, questioning, and interpreting information. The children worked alongside her, thinking aloud as she did. Asking them questions about the rotation of the spiral when the heat lamp was turned off and on engaged them in her scientific approach. She asked them what made the wind in this case. They had no trouble with the idea that the lamp caused the wind, the wind consisted of moving air, and the moving air turned the spiral.

It was still a big step, however, for the children to decide that their experiments had something to say about outdoor winds. There are problems of scale: the sun might be able to cause air movement the way the lamp does, but the lamp's wind is very gentle—and vertical. And if a wind is like a balloon going down, or somebody blowing, who holds the balloon? Who blows? Anyway, on the weather map, the wind doesn't blow straight from a center of high pressure to one of low pressure (because of the rotation of the earth). For most children these questions were best left to another time.

The children were confronting the idea of a scientific model: saying that something is like something else. They were also seeing that often our understanding is only partial.

What do scientists do?
▶ *It is possible for all of the people in a community to work scientifically. The approach is not reserved for the group of people we call scientists.*

Sally suggested to the children that throughout the unit they had been practicing working scientifically. What did they think that meant? What did they think a scientist is and does? The group produced this list in Figure 4.

Sally followed up on the idea that scientists are special and clever. Was it possible for the student to work in scientific ways, as scientists do? Could they learn to work scientifically the way they learned to play a sport or a musical instrument? The children weren't sure. They put together a list of things they thought might be involved, and Sally promised to come back to it later.

Using the wind
▶ *Working in a team and using the expertise of others is common in scientific work.*

In the weather-watch theme, the children were considering ways the community uses knowledge of the weather and weather forecasts. Sally wanted the children also to think about how people use their knowledge of air and wind. To do this, she had them make parachutes and windmills. Children from a sixth-grade class helped through a cross-age tutoring arrangement. Such support parallels the way scientists work with others who have particular expertise.

A SCIENTIST IS
- knowing
- interesting
- experimental
- special
- clever
- working

WORKING SCIENTIFICALLY INVOLVES
- knowing things
- inventing things
- doing experiments
- writing books
- explaining things
- helping people

Figure 4

Making parachutes

▸ *Understanding and developing technology often involves the application of knowledge gained from working scientifically.*

The children designed and made parachutes from plastic freezer bags and attached them to little people made from clay. They released their parachutes from upstairs windows and watched them drift down. The activity provided them with another opportunity to explore the existence of air and build on their earlier work.

It was natural, during the activity, for the children to think about how the parachute could be improved. They tried different-size canopies, different loads, and different numbers of strings. Some tried putting holes in the canopy. They experimented first by simply standing on chairs and then by dropping the parachutes out the windows. Some groups worked together to make different designs, then raced them by, dropping them out the windows at the same time.

To complete the activity, the children discussed ways that parachutes are used—in sports, in war, to deliver medicines to remote places, to save pilots from crashes.

Experiments don't always do what we want

▸ *Reporting the problems and failures in investigating is an important aspect of adopting a scientific approach.*

Children ran into quite a few problems while testing their parachutes. The parachutes did not behave consistently—on one drop, this parachute would win, but on the next drop, the other. It was a long way up and down stairs to retrieve parachutes. Wind gusts and changes sometimes interfered with the experiments. Sally encouraged the children to talk about and report on their "failures" as well as their successes.

Making windmills

Again the sixth-grade class helped with the construction and planning. Some children reported in close detail the construction of their windmill. Adrian wrote:

> Today we made a windmill. How do you make one? What do you need? Get a paddle-pop stick and get a hammer and one pair of scissors. And get a colored square and get a nail. What do you do? Cut the colored paper and when you get to the next one do not fold the next one. Get the pop stick and the nail and the hammer and the stick. Hammer the nail to the colored square and to the stick.

Measuring wind speed

The children tested their windmills in different locations and soon realized they had a means of measuring wind speed. After some initial explorations, they talked about what they had found. Where did the wind seem to be fast? slow?

The children raised some of the problems: the wind changed speed, even as you were standing there watching your windmill. It wasn't just a matter of place. As well, sometimes the windmills "got stuck" and didn't turn as fast as they should.

Together with Sally, the children worked out a strategy. In groups of six, they would go to each of four different places and write down where the wind was fast and where it was slow. Then the groups would move to a second location and take measurements again. Finally, they would come back and see whether most people had the same answers.

Measuring wind direction

How could we do it?

▸ *Brainstorming and raising options are important strategies in solve problems and planning investigations in science.*

Creating options is an important part of planning. The question Sally asked was, How can we tell which way the wind is blowing? The children considered the question in groups of three, trying to think of more than one way of finding out. They drew pictures to explain their ideas.

Sally recorded the responses on a large chart (see Figure 5). She made no attempt to evaluate the different options at this stage: the objective was simply to create options.

Of these methods, the children decided that only the wind-surfer option was unsuitable for doing at school. They felt that watching the movement of trees would be the simplest and probably the best. They agreed to try this method first, as a whole-class investigation. Sally would model how such investigations could proceed, then they could try it with the other methods in small groups.

Evaluating the trees method
▶ *Scientists evaluate their work and compare different ways of doing experiments or interpreting results.*

Outside, as a single group, the children watched the movement of trees in the wind. They tried different locations, at each place comparing small trees and bigger trees. They drew and wrote about what they saw. Back in class, Sally asked them if the trees method was a good way of telling which way the wind blew. She recorded their answers (see Figure 6). This activity was an impor-

tant one. It showed us that young children can be very good at evaluating their procedures and results.

Trying other methods
At the next session, the children, in groups of three or four, chose one of the eight other methods they had suggested earlier and used it to measure wind direction. They followed the procedures they had used with the trees, trying different locations, and in each case different points in the same wind. They needed help to direct their attention to evaluating their method rather than simply measuring winds in different places.

Back in the classroom, the groups made posters about what they had done and found. For example, Mayomi reported: "The kite that we made, the tale was moving. There wasn't much wind to fly the kite. The tale was much better than the kite."

Comparing results
▶ *Choosing the most appropriate way to investigate is a key aspect of working scientifically.*

With the help of their posters, groups reported to the rest of the class. In some teams, members had different opinions about the effectiveness of their method. Sally simply allowed such differences to be expressed. With children more experienced in evaluation, she might have proceeded to debate the methods and perhaps even rank them. This choice would depend on the children's being able to separate themselves sufficiently from their method that evaluation of the method would not be taken as evaluation of themselves.

What Have We Learned?

To complete the unit, Sally returned to the question she had asked earlier, but this time couched in terms not of what scientists do, but what children do. First, the children recalled activities, episodes, and things they had learned from both themes. From there Sally asked, "So what are some of the things

---

How can we tell which way the wind is blowing?

- Fly a kite
- Make a weather vane
- Watch which way the trees and flowers blow
- Watch a wind surfer
- Tie balloons to a tree with string
- Make a paper airplane
- Put a stick in the ground with string or paper on it
- Watch the way the clouds are moving
- Make a windmill
- Watch a flag

Figure 5

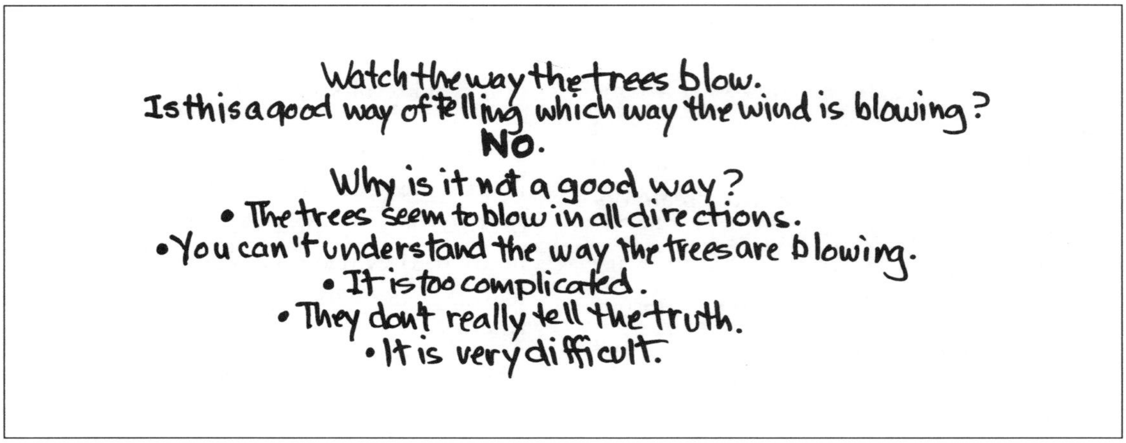

Watch the way the trees blow.
Is this a good way of telling which way the wind is blowing?
NO.
Why is it not a good way?
• The trees seem to blow in all directions.
• You can't understand the way the trees are blowing.
• It is too complicated.
• They don't really tell the truth.
• It is very difficult.

Figure 6

we do when we work scientifically?" The question was a hard one for the children, because it was asking them to abstract the skills and processes from the context of the unit. Sally allowed them to go both ways, either referring to particular things they had done ("Make a windmill to measure the wind speed") or answering more generally ("Compare different ways of measuring things").

From the children's answers, it was clear that they had developed new understanding and skills about working scientifically. It was also clear that individuals were performing at very different levels. These variations would need to be taken into account in later work.

Teacher's Reflections

We called the unit "They don't tell the truth about the wind" because of a comment by one of the children about using trees as indicators of wind direction. The comment captured the fact that young children are able to reflect critically on what they have done. This is central to the ability to work scientifically, to plan and to learn. It is exciting that many children at this level are already able, with support and encouragement, to demonstrate such thought.

Planning and teaching the unit made us much clearer about the value of modeling steps in an investigation, which the children can then imitate in their own investigations. The unit also made clear the interconnectedness of context, content, and scientific processes and of teaching and learning in science. As we worked on these links in our planning and again while teaching, we realized that effective teaching in science will always highlight such links—they are a natural part of science.